Series / Number 07-021

INTERRUPTED TIME SERIES ANALYSIS

DAVID McDOWALL
University of Michigan

RICHARD McCLEARY
Arizona State University

ERROL E. MEIDINGER
Lewis and Clark University

RICHARD A. HAY, Jr.
Northwestern University

SAGE PUBLICATIONS / Beverly Hills / London

For information address:

SAGE Publications, Inc.
275 South Beverly Drive
Beverly Hills, California 90212

SAGE Publications Ltd
28 Banner Street
London EC1Y 8QE, England

International Standard Book Number 0-8039-1493-8

Library of Congress Catalog Card No. L.C. 80-52761

FOURTH PRINTING, 1985

When citing a professional paper, please use the proper form. Remember to cite the
correct Sage University Paper series title and include the paper number. One of the
two following formats can be adapted (depending on the style manual used):

(1) IVERSEN, GUDMUND R. and NORPOTH, HELMUT (1976) "Analysis of Variance." Sage University Paper series on Quantitative Applications in the Social
Sciences, 07-001. Beverly Hills and London: Sage Pubns.

OR

(2) Iversen, Gudmund R. and Norpoth, Helmut. 1976. *Analysis of Variance.* Sage
University Paper series on Quantitative Applications in the Social Sciences, series no.
07-001. Beverly Hills and London: Sage Publications.

CONTENTS

To Cook and Campbell

Editor's Introduction

INTERRUPTED TIME SERIES ANALYSIS by David McDowall, Richard McCleary, Errol E. Meidinger, and Richard A. Hay, Jr., presents a set of techniques for the analysis of the impact of interventions upon single time series of data. It complements well one of the earlier papers in the series, TIME SERIES ANALYSIS by Charles W. Ostrom, Jr. The reader should either be knowledgeable about elementary time series techniques or should study the Ostrom volume carefully before attempting to read this paper. In addition, it would be helpful if the reader also has a working knowledge of regression analysis and algebra before undertaking this paper. For an explication of regression analysis, see another paper in this series, APPLIED REGRESSION: AN INTRODUCTION by Michael Lewis-Beck.

Interrupted time series techniques, sometimes known as quasi-experimental time series analysis, require the development of models of the process underlying a time series of data. In the first part of this paper, McDowall et al. describe how the reader would go about modeling a single time series of data using the general class of ARIMA models. The elements of ARIMA models are introduced in a straightforward manner so that a reader can easily understand the arithmetic and components of ARIMA models. The authors then move to discuss the various types of ARIMA models that can be developed and describe how these models can be used to remove the systematic component of errors in time series. Techniques for differencing and identification of models are presented in lucid detail. Once the identification of the models is complete, McDowall et al. move on to discuss the estimation and diagnosis of ARIMA models. They introduce the reader to nonlinear techniques for estimation and to how residual analysis can be employed to assess the statistical adequacy of models. In their presentation of an explicit strategy for model building, they illustrate the techniques in a step-by-step fashion using a time series of data from Chicago's Hyde Park neighborhood on purse snatchings. They then use the same data to demonstrate how seasonal models can be identified, estimated, and diagnosed using the ARIMA techniques. By the time the reader has completed this first part of the paper, the reader should have a clear understanding of how to employ ARIMA techniques to model different single time series of data.

The second part of the paper focuses upon how estimated ARIMA models can then be used to assess the impact of external interventions on time series of data. Here the authors introduce an intervention component into their time series models and show how hypotheses about various types of interventions can be tested. Using examples, they demonstrate how to specify the form of intervention effects and how to test their statistical significance. Abrupt, permanent and abrupt, temporary interventions are contrasted with gradual, permanent interventions. Specific techniques are presented to model and assess these interventions, and a strategy is outlined for the testing of rival hypotheses about these interventions. The paper concludes by discussing the various software packages that are available for interrupted time series modeling and their relative usefulness for learning the time series techniques described in this paper.

The interrupted time series techniques outlined by the authors can be employed appropriately in a number of the social science disciplines. In particular,

• political scientists might find them appropriate for assessing the impact of changes in laws that govern the behavior of individuals

• economists might use them for determining whether changes in credit controls produce changes in the borrowing behavior of businesses and consumers

• sociologists might find these techniques useful for evaluating how income maintenance experiments affect the behavior of individuals participating in welfare program

• historians might employ them to assess whether major historical events had an impact on the behavior of people experiencing those events

• psychologists and educators might wish to use these techniques to test and measure the impacts of treatments in quasi-experimental settings where more conventional experimental techniques would be inappropriate.

There are, of course, other disciplines and many other sets of problems which can employ the techniques outlined in this paper on interrupted time series analysis. Many readers will be stimulated by this paper to think of new application of these techniques in their respective disciplines. The McDowall et al. paper provides and excellent introduction to interrupted time series techniques and a firm foundation for the reader's actual use of these techniques.

—Ronald E. Weber, Editorial Board

1.0 INTRODUCTION

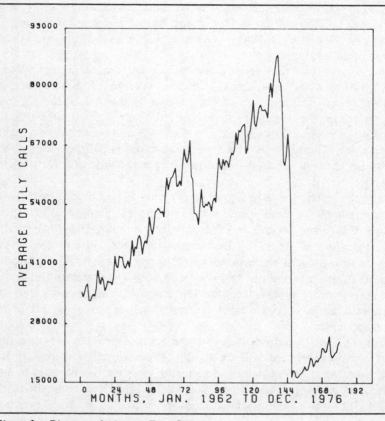

Figure 1a   Directory Assistance Time Series

The time series quasi-experiment was proposed initially by Campbell (1963; Campbell and Stanley, 1966) as a means of assessing the impact of a discrete intervention on a social process. Using the conventional Campbell-Stanley notation, the time series quasi-experiment can be diagramed as

... O O O O O O O X O O O O O O O ...

Here each O denotes an observation of a time series while the X denotes a discrete intervention. The intervention breaks the time series into two segments, one preintervention and one postintervention. As an illustration of quasi-experimental logic, consider the time series shown in Figure 1a. These data are the average daily number of calls to Cincinnati Directory Assistance recorded each month from January 1962 to December 1976 (McSweeny, 1978). In March 1974, the 147th month of this series, Cincinnati Bell initiated a $.20 charge for each call to Directory Assistance. There was no charge for these calls prior to this time. This change in policy is an example of an *intervention* and the impact of this intervention on the time series is visually striking. In the 147th month, the level of the series drops abruptly and profoundly.

The analysis of a time series quasi-experiment ordinarily focuses on a test of the null hypothesis; that is, did the intervention have an impact on the time series? The null hypothesis is tested by comparing the pre- and postintervention segments of the time series. There is no question that the intervention impacted this series, so a test of the null hypothesis may seem unnecessary. The analysis of a time series quasi-experiment can nevertheless be used in this case to estimate the magnitude and form of the impact.

The time series shown in Figure 1b presents a less obvious case. These data are workforce totals (total number of people employed) for Sutter County, California, recorded each month from January 1946 to December 1966 (Friesema et al., 1979). In January 1955, the 121st month of this series, a flood forced the evacuation of Sutter County. This is another example of an intervention. Did the flood have an impact on this series? This case is more typical than the Directory Assistance case. Here the analysis of a time series quasi-experiment will center on a test of the null hypothesis.

Both of these examples illustrate the type of problem where a time series quasi-experiment will be useful. Time series quasi-experiments have been used, for example, to test and measure the impacts of new traffic laws (Campbell and Ross, 1968; Glass, 1968; Ross et al., 1970); the impacts of decriminalization (Aaronson et al., 1978; McCleary and

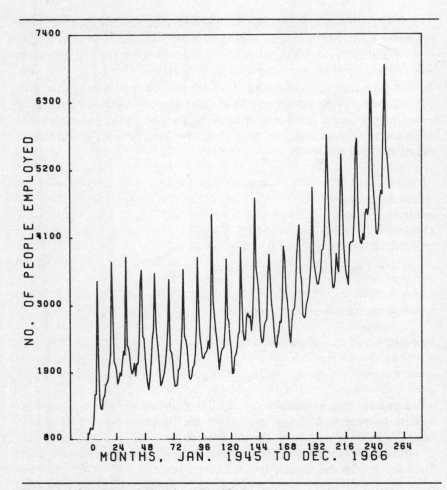

Figure 1b   Sutter County Workforce Time Series

Musheno, 1980); the impacts of gun control laws (Deutsch and Alt, 1977; Hay and McCleary, 1979; Zimring, 1975); and the impact of air pollution control laws (Box and Tiao, 1975). The widest use of this method has clearly been in the area of legal impact assessment. Time series quasi-experiments have also been used, however, by experimental psychologists to test and measure the impacts of treatments (Gottman and McFall, 1972; Hall et al., 1971; Tyler and Brown, 1968) and by political scientists to test and measure the impacts of political realignments (Caporaso and Pelowski, 1971; Lewis-Beck, 1979; Smoker, 1969).

This list is representative but by no means exhaustive. All of these examples have two things in common. First, the social process under study has been operationalized as a time series; second, there is a discrete intervention; that is, the intervention divides the time series into two distinct segments, one consisting of all preintervention observations and one consisting of all postintervention observations. Analysis of the time series quasi-experiment is a statistical comparison of the pre- and postintervention time series segments. The analysis requires a statistical model which, in this case, might be

$$Y_t = b_{pre} + b_{post} + e_t$$

where

Y_t = the tth observation of a time series

b_{pre} = the preintervention series level

b_{post} = the postintervention series level

e_t = an error term associated with Y_t.

The null hypothesis for this model,

$$H_0: b_{pre} - b_{post} = 0,$$

states that there is no statistically significant difference between the pre- and postintervention series levels, that the intervention had no statistically significant impact on the series level.

An immediate problem is the validity of this statistical conclusion. Put simply, how can the model parameters be estimated? When the time series quasi-experiment was first proposed, a number of researchers used ordinary least-squares regression estimates of the pre- and postintervention time series levels to test the null hypothesis. Ordinary least-squares regression estimates assume that adjacent error terms are uncorrelated, that is,

$$covariance(e_t e_{t-1}) = 0.$$

This assumption is seldom satisfied by time series data, however, and when error terms are correlated, the standard errors of ordinary least-squares parameter estimates are *biased*. As a result of this bias in standard errors, t statistics used to test the null hypothesis may seriously overstate the statistical significance of an impact. In the past, the conventional wisdom on this point seemed to be that, if a t statistic was "large enough," serially correlated errors would not present a strong threat to statistical conclusion validity. This conventional wisdom is incorrect. In many social science time series, serially correlated errors may inflate the standard errors of ordinary least-squares parameter estimates by 50%; the common t statistic is thus inflated by 300% or 400%; and, as a result, the statistical significance of an impact is vastly overstated. In many situations, a statistically *in*significant difference between pre- and postintervention series levels could actually have a t statistic as high as 6.0. For this reason alone, the time series quasi-experiment should not be analyzed by means of an ordinary least-squares regression model.

There are a number of statistical models which can be used to control this threat to statistical conclusion validity. If the structure of serial dependence is known, for example, the difference between pre- and post-intervention series levels may be estimated from a *generalized* least-squares model (see, e.g., Hibbs, 1974; Ostrom, 1978: 53). The structure of serial dependence is seldom known, however, so generalized least-squares models are of limited use.

A more practical approach is to empirically *model* serial dependence as a time series process. Once modeled, serial dependence is statistically controlled, so the difference between pre- and postintervention series levels may be estimated and tested for statistical significance in a straight-forward manner. A time series model of this sort might be denoted as

$$Y_t = N_t + I_t.$$

Here N_t denotes a "noise" component and I_t denotes an "intervention" component. The sense of this model is that the Y_t times series is composed of noise (or "errors") plus intervention.

Returning to Figure 1b, the Sutter County Workforce series, it appears that there is no intervention and, hence, that the series is composed of noise only. If there is an intervention, it is certainly not so visually obvious as the one in the Directory Assistance time series (Figure 1a). An intervention need not be visually obvious, however. In any time series, there may be three sources of noise which could obscure the intervention. These are:

(1) *trend:* note that this series drifts upward throughout most of its history

(2) *seasonality:* note that the series "spikes" every 12 months (This is seasonality.)

(3) *random error:* if this time series was detrended and deseasonalized, observations would still fluctuate randomly about some mean level.

Trend and seasonality, which are quite common in social science time series, and random error tend to obscure any intervention. If the model does *not* account for these types of noise, the analysis will be confounded. The postintervention level of the Sutter County Workforce series, for example, is much higher than the preintervention level. This is due only to trend. If the model did not account for this trend, an analysis of the time series quasi-experiment might incorrectly show that the flood increased the level of employment in Sutter County. Seasonality may similarly confound the analysis. Finally, each observation of this series has a random error, or shock, which makes the series somewhat unpredictable. As noted, adjacent error terms tend to be correlated and the model must account for this type of noise also. The general class of *Auto*Regressive *I*ntegrated *M*oving *A*verage (ARIMA) models we will develop in this essay account for all three types of "noise." Once these sources of variance have been modeled, the impact of an intervention can be tested and measured.

ARIMA time series models are due largely to the work of Box and Jenkins (1976). While the separate elements of ARIMA models and methods may be traced back over 50 years, Box and Jenkins must be credited with drawing the elements together into a comprehensive general model. The use of ARIMA models for analyzing time series quasi-experiments is due to work of Box and Tiao (1965, 1975). Social scientists, however, may be more familiar with the work of Glass et al. (1975) who first introduced these methods to the social sciences. Glass et al. also developed and distributed a computer program for the analysis of time series quasi-experiments (Bower et al., 1974). While the modeling procedures we develop in this essay are substantially different than the procedures outlined by Glass et al., our development owes much to their pioneering work.

The bulk of this essay deals with the methods used to build ARIMA models. Model building requires a knowledge of ARIMA algebra. ARIMA algebra is based on common statistical concepts (means, variance, and the Normal distribution), so any reader who has completed an introductory course in social statistics will have the background required for this material.

Sections 2.0 to 2.8 deal with both the algebra of ARIMA models (theory) and the empirical procedures of ARIMA model building (practice). For the general model written as

$$Y_t = N_t + I_t,$$

the N_t component is an ARIMA noise model. This N_t component serves as the null case for the time series quasi-experiment. The intervention component, I_t, is then added to the ARIMA noise component. Sections 3.0 to 3.4 deal with the algebra of the intervention component (theory) and with the practical issues of estimating and interpreting the component.

Our experiences as teachers of time series analysis (at both the graduate and undergraduate levels) convince us that this material can be learned best when theory and practice are integrated. The example time series we analyze in this essay are listed in an appendix. The reader should replicate our example analyses and, hopefully, should try to analyze other time series data. This will require access to time series software. In Section 4.0, we discuss several software packages currently available at academic computing centers.

2.0 THE STOCHASTIC COMPONENT, N_t

An observed time series, denoted as

$$Y_1, Y_2, \ldots, Y_{t-1}, Y_t$$

can be described as the *realization* of a stochastic process. Because the generating process is stochastic, it could have generated many time series. The observed time series is thus only one *realization* of the process. If we understand how the process operates, however, we can build a model for it. Using this model to control for process noise (trend, seasonality, and so forth), we can assess the impact of an intervention. This is the basic idea of ARIMA modeling. An ARIMA model is a model of the stochastic process which generated the observed time series. At heart of this generating process is a sequence of random shocks, a_t, which conveniently summarize the multitude of factors producing the variation observed in the series. In order to model a time series process, we must make some assumptions about the behavior of these shocks. Specifically, we require

(1) zero mean for the shocks: mean(a_t) = 0
(2) constant variance for the shocks: variance(a_t) = σ^2
(3) independent shocks: covariance($a_t a_{t+k}$) = 0.

In addition, the models we will consider in this essay require one further assumption:

(4) the Normal distribution for the shocks: $a_t \sim N$.

In other words, the random shocks are Normally, independently, and identically distributed with zero mean and constant variance.

An ARIMA model has three structural parameters, p, d, and q, which describe the relationships between random shocks and the time series. The structural parameter p indicates an *autoregressive* relationship. For example, an ARIMA(1,0,0) model (p = 1, d = q = 0) is written as

$$Y_t = \phi_1 Y_{t-1} + a_t.$$

An ARIMA(1,0,0) model is one where the current time series observation, Y_t, is composed of a portion of the preceding observation, Y_{t-1}, and a random shock, a_t. An ARIMA(2,0,0) model would be written as

$$Y_t = \phi_1 Y_{t-1} + \phi_2 Y_{t-2} + a_t.$$

The parameter p thus denotes the number of autoregressive structures in the model (the number of past observations used to predict the current observation, that is). The structural parameter q denotes the number of moving average structures in the model. An ARIMA(0,0,1) model would thus be written as

$$Y_t = a_t - \theta_1 a_{t-1}$$

and an ARIMA(0,0,2) model would be written as

$$Y_t = a_t - \theta_1 a_{t-1} - \theta_2 a_{t-2}.$$

An ARIMA(0,0,q) model is one where the current time series observation, Y_t, is composed of a current random shock, a_t, and portions of the q-1 preceding random shocks, a_{t-1} through a_{t-q}. Finally, the structural parameter d indicates that the time series was *differenced*. Differencing amounts to subtracting the first observation of the series from the second observation, the second observation from the third, and so on. An ARIMA (0,1,0) model would be written as

$$Y_t - Y_{t-1} = a_t$$

$$Y_t = Y_{t-1} + a_t$$

and, of course, the *differenced* time series may be set equal in the model to an autoregressive or moving average. An ARIMA(0,1,1) model, for example, would be written as

$$Y_t - Y_{t-1} = a_t - \theta_1 a_{t-1}$$

$$Y_t = Y_{t-1} + a_t - \theta_1 a_{t-1}.$$

The sense of this ARIMA(0,1,1) model is that the current time series observation, Y_t, is equal to the preceding observation, Y_{t-1}, plus the current random shock, a_t, and plus a portion of the preceding random shock, a_{t-1}.

Identification refers to the empirical procedures by which the best or most appropriate set of structural parameters (the most appropriate values for p, d, and q, that is) are selected for a given time series. In general, the analyst will have to know how many times to difference the data (d) and how many autoregressive and/or moving average parameters to estimate for a set of data (p and q). We will begin describing these identification procedures in the next section. First, however, a description of the random shock, a_t, is in order.

The basis of an ARIMA(p,d,q) process is a sequence of random shocks, or a "white noise" process. The tth observation of a "white noise" process, a_t, is randomly and independently drawn from a normal distribution with zero-mean and constant variance, σ^2. It may be helpful to think of white noise shocks as the *input* to an ARIMA(p,d,q) model. This can be diagramed as

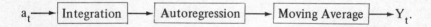

$$a_t \longrightarrow \boxed{\text{Integration}} \longrightarrow \boxed{\text{Autoregression}} \longrightarrow \boxed{\text{Moving Average}} \longrightarrow Y_t.$$

The sense of this diagram is that a random shock enters the ARIMA model, passes through a sequence of "filters," and leaves the ARIMA model as a time series observation. This input-output scheme is central to ARIMA algebra. The sequence of "filters," or "black boxes," are ARIMA structures which determine the properties of the output time series, Y_t: integration or differencing (d), autoregression (p), and moving average (q).

In the next section, we will develop the algebra of the various ARIMA structures and demonstrate an empirical strategy for building an ARIMA (p,d,q) model for a time series. All of this material can be explained in terms of the white noise inputs and time series outputs of an ARIMA model (or filter or black box). In general, the ARIMA model is a system of filters that determines the properties of the output series, Y_t. An ARIMA(0,1,1) model, for example, describes a system where the random shock input passes through a differencing filter and a moving average filter but not through an autoregression filter. Similarly, an ARIMA(1,0,1) model describes a system where the random shock input passes through autoregression and moving average filters but not through a differencing filter. As we will demonstrate, the outputs of these two systems are quite different.

2.1 ARIMA(0,0,0) and ARIMA(0,d,0) Processes

An ARIMA(0,0,0) process is simply a sequence of random shocks. Such a process may be written as

$$Y_t = a_t.$$

Where Y_t is a time series observation and a_t a random shock. Successive realizations of this process are

$$Y_0 = Y_0$$
$$Y_1 = a_1$$

$$Y_t = a_t.$$

This ARIMA(0,0,0) process generates time series observations that fluctuate noisily about a zero mean. A slightly more complicated version of the ARIMA(0,0,0) process is

$$Y_t = \theta_0 + a_t,$$

where θ_0 is a parameter to be estimated. The difference between these two ARIMA(0,0,0) processes is that, in the first case, the mean or level of the series is zero. In the second case, the level of the series is some nonzero constant, θ_0.

It will be instructive here to describe both processes as input-output systems. In the first case, the ARIMA(0,0,0) system is

$$a_t \longrightarrow Y_t.$$

The sense of this diagram is that the random shock input passes through *no* filters. In the second case,

$$a_t \longrightarrow \boxed{+\theta_0} \longrightarrow Y_t.$$

The sense of this diagram is that the random shock enters a filter where a constant, θ_0, is added. The output of the filter is the time series observation, Y_t. In either case, however, the model implies a flat noisy type of stochastic behavior, "white noise."

A slightly more complicated ARIMA process is realized when the random shocks are *integrated* or summed. For example, consider the process where successive observations are

$$Y_0 = Y_0$$
$$Y_1 = Y_0 + a_1$$
$$Y_2 = Y_0 + a_1 + a_2$$
$$Y_3 = Y_0 + a_1 + a_2 + a_3$$

$$Y_t = Y_0 + a_1 + a_2 + \ldots + a_{t-1} + a_t.$$

This process is called a "random walk." Each realization of the process consists of all past random shocks *integrated* (or summed) with a "starting value," Y_0, into a single observation.

Although white noise and integrated processes are based on the same random shocks inputs, the two processes imply radically different stochastic behaviors, or outputs. While the ARIMA(0,0,0) process has a flat appearance, for example, integrated processes will *trend* or *drift*. Trend is motion in a specific direction, usually (to simplify matters) upward or downward. More specifically, trend is defined as *any systematic change in the level of a time series process.* An integrated process follows a trend whenever the white noise input process has a nonzero mean. For example, let

$$\text{mean}(a_t) = \theta_0$$

where θ_0 is a nonzero constant. Then successive realizations of the integrated process are expected to be

$$Y_0 = Y_0$$
$$Y_1 = Y_0 + \text{mean}(a_1)$$
$$= Y_0 + \theta_0$$
$$Y_2 = Y_0 + \text{mean}(a_1) + \text{mean}(a_2)$$
$$= Y_0 + 2\theta_0$$
$$Y_3 = Y_0 + \text{mean}(a_1) + \text{mean}(a_2) + \text{mean}(a_3)$$
$$= Y_0 + 3\theta_0$$

$$Y_t = Y_0 + \text{mean}(a_1) + \text{mean}(a_2) + \ldots + \text{mean}(a_{t-1}) + \text{mean}(a_t)$$

$$= Y_0 + t\theta_0.$$

So the level of the process is expected to increase or decrease (depending upon whether θ_0 is positive or negative) with each successive observation. The constant θ_0 in this case is interpreted as the *slope* of the process.

Even when the random shocks have a zero mean, however, the integrated process will not have flat realizations. Figure 2.1a shows a time series of 369 daily price quotations for IBM common stock (Box and Jenkins, 1976: 526-527). As we will demonstrate in the next section, this series is the realization of an integrated process where the expected value of the random shocks are zero. While the process does not follow a trend, it *drifts*, first upward and then downward. In practice, it is often difficult to distinguish drift from trend. If only the first half of this series were available, the analyst might conclude that the process follows an upward trend. If only the second half of this series were available, on the other hand, the analyst might conclude exactly the opposite, that the process follows a downward trend. In fact, however, when the entire series is available, the analyst would conclude that the process follows no trend whatsoever, but instead drifts stochastically.

Whether the integrated process trends or drifts, it may be represented by an ARIMA(0,d,0) model. For this class of models, the structural parameter d indicates that the time series has been *differenced*. Differencing transforms a process that trends or drifts into one that neither trends nor drifts. To demonstrate the practical consequences of differencing a time series, consider the integrated process

$$Y_0 = Y_0$$

$$Y_1 = Y_0 + a_1$$

$$Y_2 = Y_0 + a_1 + a_2$$

$$Y_t = Y_0 + a_1 + a_2 + \ldots + a_{t-1} + a_t.$$

If this process is *differenced*, that is, if the first observation is subtracted from the second, the second from the third, and so forth,

$$Y_1 - Y_0 = Y_0 + a_1 - Y_0$$

$$= a_1$$

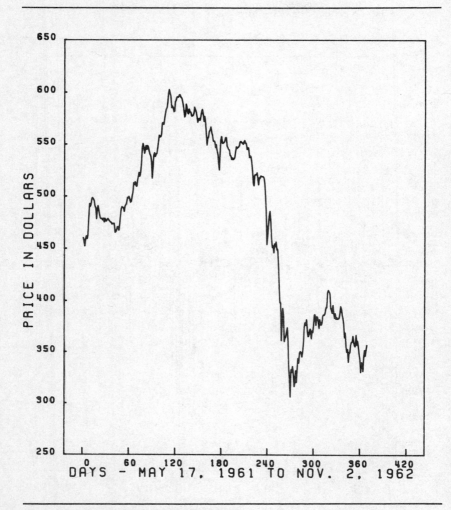

Figure 2.1a The IBM Stock Price Time Series

$$Y_2 - Y_1 \quad = Y_0 + a_1 + a_2 - Y_0 - a_1$$
$$= a_2$$

$$Y_3 - Y_2 \quad = Y_0 + a_1 + a_2 + a_3 - Y_0 - a_1 - a_2$$
$$= a_3$$

$$Y_t - Y_{t-1} = Y_0 + a_1 + \ldots + a_t - Y_0 - a_1 - \ldots - a_{t-1}$$
$$= a_t,$$

22

the differenced time series is white noise.

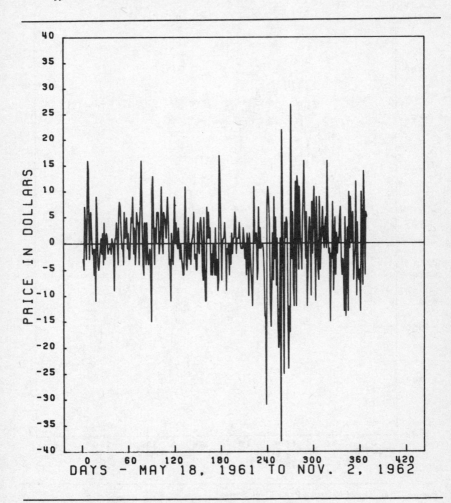

Figure 2.1b   The IBM Stock Price Time Series, Differenced

Figure 2.1b shows the differenced IBM stock price time series. Whereas prior to differencing the series drifted up and down throughout its course, after differencing the series fluctuates noisily about a mean of zero. This time series is thus well represented by an ARIMA(0,1,0) model where d = 1 indicates that one differencing was required to transform the series from nonstationarity (drifting behavior) to stationarity (nondrifting behavior).

Finally, it will be instructive to diagram the ARIMA(0,1,0) process as an input-output system. First, the random shock enters a filter where a constant is added.

$$a_t \longrightarrow \boxed{+\theta_0} \longrightarrow (a_t + \theta_0).$$

Second, the $(a_t + \theta_0)$ shock enters a filter where it is *integrated* with all past shocks.

$$(a_t + \theta_0) \longrightarrow \boxed{+ \sum_{i=1}^{\infty} (a_{t-i} + \theta_0)} \longrightarrow Y_t.$$

The output is the time series observation, Y_t. Of course, if the constant θ_0 is zero, the Y_t process is a "random walk"; if θ_0 is nonzero, Y_t follows a linear trend.

In this diagram, we have indicated an integration back into the *infinite* past and, of course, this cannot be done with a finite time series. However, the starting value of the time series is the sum of all historical shocks.

$$Y_0 = \sum_{i=0}^{\infty} a_{t-i}$$

and

$$Y_t = \sum_{i=0}^{t-1} a_{t-i} + Y_0$$

therefore

$$Y_t = \sum_{i=0}^{\infty} a_{t-i}$$

which is consistent with the notation used in the filter diagram.

The reader is urged to become familiar with the notion of inputs, outputs, and filters. This input-output analogy gives a simple description of even the most complicated and cumbersome ARIMA model. While the mathematics of time series analysis may sometimes be difficult to grasp, the common sense basis of time series analysis, stated in input-output terms, will be surprisingly easy to grasp. At its basis, a time series *process* consists of random shock or white noise *inputs* and realization or observation *outputs*. Between input and output, are a series of filters which shape a shock (a_t) into a realization (Y_t). The ARIMA(0,0,0) and ARIMA (0,d,0) filters described here are typical examples. After a short digression, we will consider the ARIMA(p,0,0) and ARIMA(0,0,q) filters which shape the inputs into autoregressive and moving average outputs.

2.2 The Autocorrelation Function

A *stationary* stochastic process (one that neither trends nor drifts) is fully determined by its mean, variance, and *autocorrelation function* (ACF). If two processes have the same mean, variance, and ACF, then they are the same process. Because each distinct process has a distinct ACF, we can estimate an ACF from a realized time series and use that information to determine the process structure which generated the realization.

For a Y_t time series process, the ACF is defined as

$$ACF(k) = covariance(Y_t Y_{t+k}) / variance(Y_t).$$

Given a realization of the Y_t process, a finite time series of N observations, the ACF may be estimated from the formula

$$ACF(k) = \frac{\sum_{i=1}^{N} (Y_i - Y)(Y_{i+k} - Y)}{\sum_{i=1}^{N} (Y_i - Y)^2} \left(\frac{N}{N-k}\right)$$

ACF(k) is thus a measure of correlation between Y_t and Y_{t+k}. To illustrate the formula for estimating ACF(k), lag the Y_t series forward in time:

lag-0 Y_1 Y_2 Y_3 ... Y_N

lag-1 Y_1 Y_2 ... Y_{N-1} Y_N

lag-2 Y_1 ... Y_{N-2} Y_{N-1} Y_N

and so forth. ACF(1) is the correlation coefficient estimated between the time series (lag-0) and its first lag (lag-1); ACF(2) is the correlation coefficient estimated between the time series (lag-0) and its second lag (lag-2); and in general, ACF(k) is the correlation coefficient estimated between the time series (lag-0) and its kth lag (lag-k). For each lag, one pair of observations is lost from the estimate of ACF(k). ACF(1) is estimated from N-1 pairs of observations; ACF(2) is estimated from N-2 pairs of observations and so forth. As the value of k increases, confidence in the estimate of ACF(k) diminishes.

In theory, each type of ARIMA(p,d,q) process has a unique ACF. For example, the ARIMA(0,0,0) process written as $Y_t = a_t$ is expected to have a uniformly zero ACF. That is,

$$ACF(1) = ACF(2) = \ldots = ACF(k) = 0.$$

This follows from the definition of the random shocks which constitute the ARIMA(0,0,0) process; each shock is independent of every other shock. Observations of the process are thus uncorrelated. In contrast, an ARIMA(0,1,0) process written as

$$Y_t = Y_{t-1} + a_t$$

or

$$Y_t - Y_{t-1} = a_t$$

is expected to have a large value of ACF(1) and successive lags of the ACF are expected to die out slowly to zero. That is,

$$ACF(1) \approx 1$$

$$ACF(k-1) \approx ACF(k).$$

This follows from the definition of the ARIMA(0,1,0) process:

$$Y_t = Y_0 + a_1 + \ldots + a_{t-1} + a_t.$$

The neighboring observations, Y_t and Y_{t+1}, are identical except for one random shock. Similarly, the observations Y_t and Y_{t+2} are identical except for two random shocks. Two observations of the integrated process will thus *always* be correlated to some extent but the correlation will decrease as the distance between the two observations increases.

Figure 2.2a shows the ACF estimated from the IBM stock price time series. In the previous section, we stated without proof that this time series was the realization of an ARIMA(0,1,0) process. Here we present the ACF

```
SERIES. .  IBM   (NOBS= 369)    IBM STOCK CLOSINGS
NO. OF VALID OBSERVATIONS =      369.

AUTOCORRELATIONS OF LAGS 1 - 25


   LAG    CORR    SE   -1   -.8  -.6  -.4  -.2   Ø    .2   .4   .6   .8  +1
                       +----+----+----+----+----+----+----+----+----+----+
    1    .993   .Ø5Ø                              ( IX)XXXXXXXXXXXXXXXXXXXXXX
    2    .986   .Ø9Ø                             (   IXXX)XXXXXXXXXXXXXXXXXXXX
    3    .978   .12Ø                           (     IXXXXX)XXXXXXXXXXXXXXXXXX
    4    .971   .14Ø                          (      IXXXXXX)XXXXXXXXXXXXXXXXX
    5    .964   .15Ø                         (       IXXXXXX)XXXXXXXXXXXXXXXXX
    6    .956   .17Ø                        (        IXXXXXXX)XXXXXXXXXXXXXXXX
    7    .948   .18Ø                       (         IXXXXXXXX)XXXXXXXXXXXXXXX
    8    .939   .2ØØ                      (          IXXXXXXXXX)XXXXXXXXXXXXXX
    9    .93Ø   .21Ø                      (          IXXXXXXXXX)XXXXXXXXXXXXXX
   1Ø    .922   .22Ø                     (           IXXXXXXXXXX)XXXXXXXXXXXXX
   11    .914   .23Ø                    (            IXXXXXXXXXXX)XXXXXXXXXXX
   12    .9Ø5   .24Ø                    (            IXXXXXXXXXXX)XXXXXXXXXXX
   13    .897   .25Ø                    (            IXXXXXXXXXXX)XXXXXXXXXXX
   14    .889   .26Ø                   (             IXXXXXXXXXXXX)XXXXXXXXXX
   15    .881   .26Ø                   (             IXXXXXXXXXXXX)XXXXXXXXXX
   16    .872   .27Ø                   (             IXXXXXXXXXXXX)XXXXXXXXX
   17    .863   .28Ø                  (              IXXXXXXXXXXXXX)XXXXXXXX
   18    .853   .29Ø                  (              IXXXXXXXXXXXXX)XXXXXXXX
   19    .841   .29Ø                  (              IXXXXXXXXXXXXX)XXXXXXXX
   2Ø    .832   .3ØØ                 (               IXXXXXXXXXXXXXX)XXXXXX
   21    .821   .31Ø                 (               IXXXXXXXXXXXXXX)XXXXXX
   22    .81Ø   .31Ø                 (               IXXXXXXXXXXXXXX)XXXXXX
   23    .799   .32Ø                (                IXXXXXXXXXXXXXXX)XXXX
   24    .789   .32Ø                (                IXXXXXXXXXXXXXXX)XXXX
   25    .775   .33Ø                (                IXXXXXXXXXXXXXXX)XXXX
                            -2SE                                +2SE
```

Figure 2.2a   ACF for the Raw IBM Stock Price Time Series

to back up that statement. The ACF starts with high positive values and dies out slowly to zero. This is solid evidence for a *nonstationary* process of which the ARIMA(0,1,0) is one case. Figure 2.2b shows the ACF estimated from the *differenced* IBM series. This ACF is effectively zero for all lags, indicating that the differenced series is the realization of a white noise or ARIMA(0,0,0) process.

Figures 2.2a and 2.2b are the output of SCRUNCH (Hay, 1979), a computer program designed especially for Box-Tiao time series analyses. The parentheses about each lag of the ACF are 95% confidence intervals. Standard errors for the estimated value of ACF(k) are given by the formula

$$SE[ACF(k)] = \sqrt{1/N \left(1 + 2 \sum_{i=1}^{k} ACF(i)^2\right)}$$

```
SERIES. . IBM   (NOBS=  369)  IBM STOCK CLOSINGS
DIFFERENCED  1 TIME(S) OF ORDER  1.
NO. OF VALID OBSERVATIONS  =   368.

AUTOCORRELATIONS OF LAGS 1 - 25.


LAG   CORR    SE  -1  -.8  -.6  -.4  -.2   Ø   .2   .4   .6   .8  +1
                  +----+----+----+----+----+----+----+----+----+----+
  1   .Ø86   .Ø5Ø                         ( IX)
  2  -.ØØ1   .Ø5Ø                         ( I )
  3  -.Ø54   .Ø5Ø                         (XI )
  4  -.Ø35   .Ø5Ø                         (XI )
  5  -.Ø24   .Ø5Ø                         ( I )
  6   .121   .Ø5Ø                         ( IX)X
  7   .Ø68   .Ø5Ø                         ( IX)
  8   .Ø36   .Ø5Ø                         ( IX)
  9  -.Ø66   .Ø5Ø                         (XI )
 1Ø   .Ø22   .Ø5Ø                         ( I )
 11   .Ø77   .Ø5Ø                         ( IX)
 12   .Ø54   .Ø5Ø                         ( IX)
 13  -.Ø48   .Ø5Ø                         (XI )
 14   .Ø66   .Ø5Ø                         ( IX)
 15  -.Ø66   .Ø5Ø                         (XI )
 16   .119   .Ø6Ø                         ( IX*
 17   .125   .Ø6Ø                         ( IX)X
 18   .Ø52   .Ø6Ø                         ( IX)
 19   .Ø49   .Ø6Ø                         ( IX)
 2Ø   .Ø66   .Ø6Ø                         ( IX)
 21  -.Ø87   .Ø6Ø                         (XI )
 22  -.Ø31   .Ø6Ø                         ( I )
 23   .Ø64   .Ø6Ø                         ( IX)
 24   .Ø31   .Ø6Ø                         ( I )
 25   .Ø2Ø   .Ø6Ø                         ( I )
                                      -2SE    +2SE
```

Figure 2.2b   ACF for the Differenced IBM Stock Price Time Series

Estimated values of ACF(k) which lie within the ±2 standard error confidence intervals are thus not statistically different than zero at a .95 level of confidence.

2.3 Moving Average Models

In practice, time series analysis begins with an ACF estimated from the raw or undifferenced time series, Y_t. If this ACF indicates that the process is *nonstationary*, the series must be differenced. The second step of the analysis is an *identification* of an ARIMA model for the stationary series (or for a series that has been made stationary by differencing) based on the patterns of serial correlation shown in the ACF. In the previous section, the ACF estimated from the raw IBM series (Figure 2.2a) indicated that the process was nonstationary; differencing was required. The ACF estimated from the differenced IBM series (Figure 2.2b) showed no serial correlation, suggesting an ARIMA(0,0,0) model for the differenced series or, equivalently, an ARIMA(0,1,0) model for the raw series.

ARIMA(0,0,0) processes are not commonly encountered in the social sciences. More often, the ACF of the stationary series will indicate some serial dependency. One of the most common classes of serial dependency is the qth order moving average. An ARIMA(0,0,q) process is written as[1]

$$Y_t = a_t - \theta_1 a_{t-1} - \ldots - \theta_q a_{t-q}.$$

This assumes that the Y_t process is stationary, of course. If it is *non-stationary*, the ARIMA(0,1,q) process is

$$Y_t - Y_{t-1} = a_t - \theta_1 a_{t-1} - \ldots - q_q a_{t-q}.$$

The principle is nonetheless the same. A realization of the stationary process is composed of the current random shock, a_t, and portions of the q preceding random shocks, a_{t-1} through a_{t-q}. Due to this composition, consecutive realizations of a moving average process will never be independent.

In practice, social science time series are almost always well represented by lower order ARIMA(p,d,q) models. The structural parameters p, d, and q will rarely exceed the first order. Our discussion of ARIMA(0,0,q) models will thus focus on first-order cases but the arguments are general to higher order cases.

ARIMA(0,0,1) processes leave distinctive signatures in their ACFs. Writing two consecutive realizations of an ARIMA(0,0,1) process—or an ARIMA(0,1,1) process after differencing—as

$$Y_t = a_t - \theta_1 a_{t-1}$$
$$Y_{t+1} = a_{t+1} - \theta_1 a_t$$

covariance between successive observations is[2]

$$\text{covariance}(a_t a_{t+1}) = -\theta_1 \sigma^2.$$

The variance of the process can similarly be shown to be[3]

$$\text{variance}(Y_t) = (1 + \theta_1^2)\sigma^2.$$

The value of ACF(1) is thus expected to be

$$ACF(1) = \frac{-\theta_1 \sigma^2}{(1 + \theta_1^2)\sigma^2} = \frac{-\theta_1}{1 + \theta_1^2}$$

Covariance for realizations separated by two units of time is[4]

$$\text{covariance}(Y_t Y_{t+2}) = 0.$$

The value of ACF(2) is thus expected to be

$$ACF(2) = \frac{\text{covariance}(Y_t Y_{t+2})}{\text{variance}(Y_t)} = \frac{0}{1 + \theta_1^2} = 0$$

The values of ACF(3), . . . , ACF(k) are expected to be zero for the same reason. *An ARIMA(0,0,1) process is thus expected to have a nonzero value for ACF(1) and all successive lags of the ACF are expected to be zero.*

An ARIMA(0,0,2) process written as

$$Y_t = a_t - \theta_1 a_{t-1} - \theta_2 a_{t-2}$$

has a realization composed of the current random shock, a_t, and portions of the two preceding shocks, a_{t-1} and a_{t-2}. The ACF expected for this process may be derived with the same procedures used to derive the ACF expected for an ARIMA(1,0,0) process.[5]

$$ACF(1) = \frac{\theta_1(\theta_2 - 1)}{1 + \theta_1^2 + \theta_2^2}$$

$$ACF(2) = \frac{-\theta_2}{1 + \theta_1^2 + \theta_2^2}$$

$$ACF(3) = \ldots = ACF(k) = 0.$$

As a general principle, an ARIMA(0,0,q) process is expected to have non-zero values for ACF(1), . . . , ACF(q). The values of ACF(q+1), . . . , ACF(q+k) are all expected to be zero. Identification of an ARIMA (0,0,q) model is based on a count of the number of nonzero spikes in the first q lags of the ACF. In practice, of course, moving average processes higher than the first order (q > 1) will rarely be encountered.

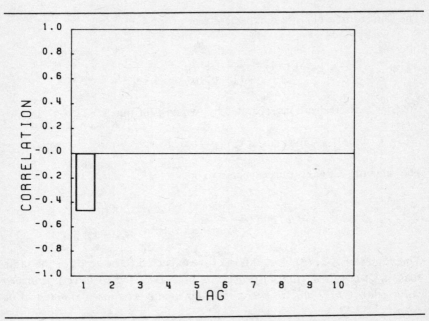

Figure 2.3   ACFs for Several ARIMA (0,0,1) and ARIMA (0,0,2) Processes
$\theta_1 = .7$

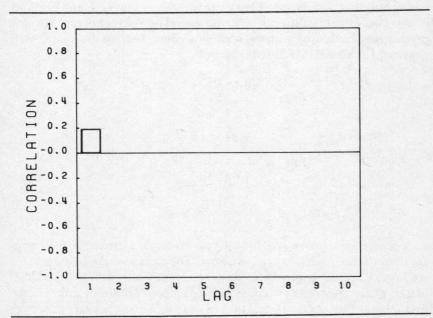

$\theta_1 = -.2$

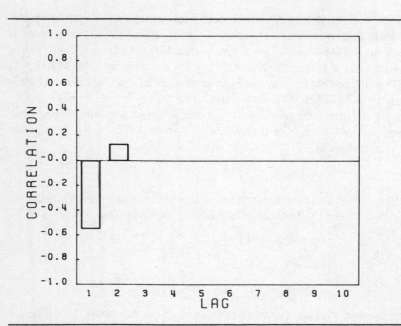

$\theta_1 = .7, \theta_2 = -.2$

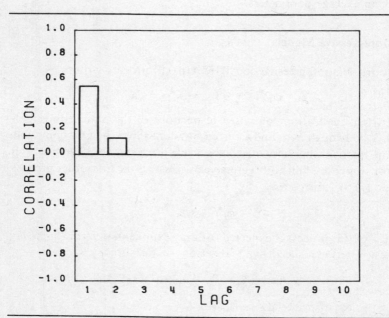

$\theta_2 = -.7, \theta_2 = -.2$

Figure 2.3 shows the ACFs expected for several ARIMA(0,0,1) and ARIMA(0,0,2) processes. These ACFs hint at the procedures used to *identify* an ARIMA model for a time series. If the ACF estimated from a time series has a single spike at ACF(1), for example, an ARIMA(0,0,1) model is suggested for the time series; spikes at ACF(1) and ACF(2) suggest an ARIMA(0,0,2) model and so forth.

Finally, it must be noted that moving average parameters are constrained to the "*bounds of invertibility*." For an ARIMA(0,0,1) process, these constraints are

$$-1 < \theta_1 < +1.$$

In other words, the parameter θ_1 must be smaller than unity in absolute value. For an ARIMA(0,0,2) process, the bounds of invertibility are

$$-1 < \theta_1 < +1$$
$$\theta_1 + \theta_2 < +1$$
$$\theta_2 - \theta_1 < +1.$$

When moving average parameters do not lie within these bounds, the ARIMA(0,0,q) model is undefined. We will return to this point in the next section to demonstrate the implications of the bounds of invertibility for moving average parameters.

2.4 Autoregressive Models

A pth order autoregressive or ARIMA(p,0,0) process written as

$$Y_t = \phi_1 Y_{t-1} + \ldots + \phi_p Y_{t-p} + a_t$$

has a current realization composed of portions of the p preceding realizations, Y_{t-1} through Y_{t-p}, and a current random shock, a_t. Our comments about the relative simplicity of social science processes apply here as well. The most common of all autoregressive processes is the first-order process, ARIMA(1,0,0), written as

$$Y_t = \phi_1 Y_{t-1} + a_t.$$

The ACF of this process is expected to decay exponentially from lag to lag. Covariance between successive realizations of the process is[5]

$$\text{covariance}(Y_t Y_{t+1}) = \phi_1 \text{variance}(Y_t).$$

Dividing this covariance by the variance of Y_t,

$$\text{ACF}(1) = \frac{\phi_1 \text{variance}(Y_t)}{\text{variance}(Y_t)} = \phi_1.$$

Covariance between realizations two units apart in time is[7]

$$\text{covariance}(Y_t Y_{t+2}) = \phi_1^2 \text{variance}(Y_t)$$

so

$$\text{ACF}(2) = \frac{\phi_1^2 \text{variance}(Y_t)}{\text{variance}(Y_t)} = \phi_1^2.$$

Continuing this procedure, it can be shown that

$$\text{ACF}(3) = \phi_1^3$$
$$\text{ACF}(4) = \phi_1^4$$

$$\text{ACF}(k) = \phi_1^k.$$

The expected ACF is thus a simple power function of the autoregressive parameter, ϕ_1.

Figure 2.4 shows the ACFs expected of ARIMA(1,0,0) processes with various values of ϕ_1. For reasons that will soon be made clear, ϕ_1 must be constrained to the interval $-1 < \phi_1 < +1$. These constraints are called the "bounds of stationarity" for a first-order autoregressive process. To demonstrate the implications of these bounds, write the ARIMA(1,0,0) process at two points in time:

$$Y_t = \phi_1 Y_{t-1} + a_t$$

and

$$Y_{t-1} = \phi_1 Y_{t-2} + a_{t-1}.$$

An obvious substitution leads to

$$Y_t = \phi_1(\phi_1 Y_{t-2} + a_{t-1}) + a_t$$

$$= \phi_1^2 Y_{t-2} + \phi_1 a_{t-1} + a_t.$$

Furthermore, an identity for Y_{t-2} is

$$Y_{t-2} = \phi_1 Y_{t-3} + a_{t-2}$$

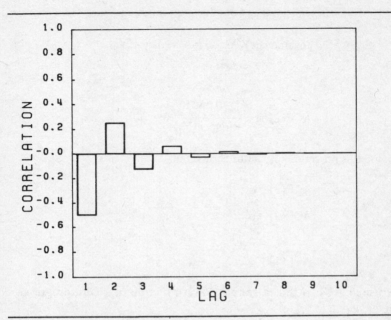

Figure 2.4 ACFs for Several ARIMA (1,0,0) Processes

$\phi_1 = -.5$

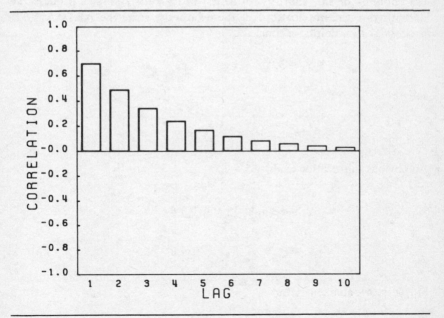

$\phi_1 = .7$

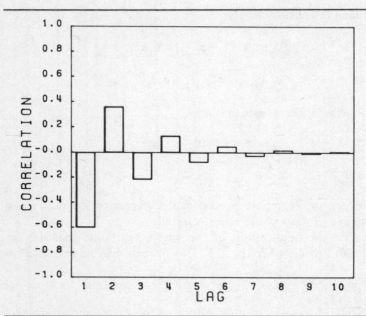

 $\phi_1 = -.6$

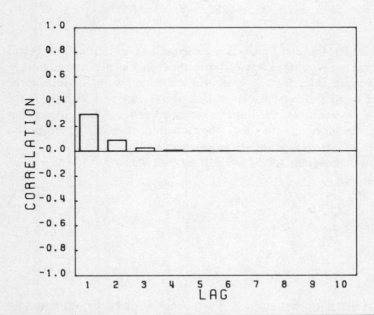

$\phi_1 = .3$

and substituting this identity leads to

$$Y_t = \phi_1^2(\phi_1 Y_{t-3} + a_{t-2}) + \phi_1 a_{t-1} + a_t$$

$$= \phi_1^3 Y_{t-3} + \phi_1^2 a_{t-2} + \phi_1 a_{t-1} + a_t.$$

Continuing this substitution back into time,

$$Y_t = \sum_{i=0}^{\infty} \phi_1^i a_{t-i}.$$

So a first-order autoregressive process can be expressed identically as a moving average process whose order is infinite.

To illustrate the implications of this important point, consider the ARIMA(1,0,0) process where $\phi_1 = .5$. This process may be expressed as

$$Y_t = \sum_{i=0}^{\infty} (.5)^i a_{t-i}$$

$$= a_t + .5 a_{t-1} + .25 a_{t-2} + .125 a_{t-3} + \ldots + (.5)^k a_{t-k} + \ldots.$$

While this ARIMA(1,0,0) process is composed of an infinite number of past shocks, the weights associated with these shocks decrease exponentially in absolute value. *This is the nature of autoregression.* So long as the parameter ϕ_1 is a fraction (that is, *so long as the value of ϕ_1 lies within the bounds of stationarity*), the importance of a random shock diminishes with time. The more recent a shock, the more important it is (or the greater its weight) in determining the current realization.

But now consider an ARIMA(1,0,0) process where $\phi_1 = 1$. The process may be written as

$$Y_t = \sum_{i=0}^{\infty} (1.0)^i a_{t-i}$$

$$= a_t + a_{t-1} + a_{t-2} + a_{t-3} + \ldots + (1.0)^k a_{t-k} + \ldots$$

which is a nonstationary process. Each shock is given the same weight regardless of how near or far in the past it is. As we demonstrated in Section 2.1, this process must be differenced.

Finally, consider an ARIMA(1,0,0) process where $\phi_1 = 1.5$. This process is

$$Y_t = a_t + 1.5a_{t-1} + 2.25a_{t-2} + \ldots + (1.5)^k a_{t-k} + \ldots.$$

In this case, a shock becomes more important as time passes. When $\phi_1 > 1$, an ARIMA(1,0,0) process implies growth. As an illustration of such a process, consider a situation where a wage earner deposits a more or less random amount of money in a savings account each month. Due to interest paid, each deposit will "grow" as time passes. After a long period of time, the earliest deposits will have grown so extemely large that the amount of money in the account will be changed little by current and future deposits. Straightforward growth processes are rare in the social sciences, however.

Nonstationary processes should not be represented by autoregressive models and, for this reason, the bounds of stationarity must be satisfied. When the parameter ϕ_1 is less than unity in absolute value, random shocks have a weaker and weaker influence as time passes. This is the distinctive nature of autoregression: The more recent an event, the greater its influence on the current realization. In input-output terms, autoregressive behavior can be diagramed as

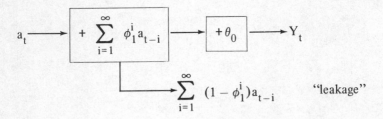

The sense of this diagram is that a random shock is added to an exponentially weighted sum of past shocks; this sum is then added to a constant, θ_0, and emerges from the ARIMA system as the current realization, Y_t. An important aspect of this diagram is its "leakage." As time passes, random shocks "leak" out of the system at an exponential rate. The influence of a random shock on a time series observation thus decreases exponentially with time. For an initial random shock, a_0, the portion remaining at successive times is:

TIME	PORTION REMAINING	LEAKAGE
$t = 0$	a_0	$\ldots$
$t = 1$	$\phi_1 a_0$	$(1 - \phi_1) a_0$
$t = 2$	$\phi_1^2 a_0$	$(1 - \phi_1^2) a_0$
$t = k$	$\phi_1^k a_0 \approx 0$	$(1 - \phi_1^k) a_0 \approx a_0.$

After k periods, the portion of a_0 remaining in the ARIMA(1,0,0) system is so small that we may think of it as zero. The portion lost through leakage is so large that we may think of it as all of a_0.

Now reconsider the bounds of invertibility for moving average parameters. Writing an ARIMA(0,0,1) process at two points in time as

$$Y_t = a_t - \theta_1 a_{t-1}$$

and

$$Y_{t-1} = a_{t-1} - \theta_1 a_{t-2},$$

an obvious substitution is

$$a_{t-1} = Y_{t-1} + \theta_1 a_{t-2}$$

so

$$Y_t = a_t - \theta_1 (Y_{t-1} + \theta_1 a_{t-2})$$

$$= a_t - \theta_1 Y_{t-1} - \theta_1^2 a_{t-2}.$$

Then substituting for a_{t-2}

$$a_{t-2} = Y_{t-2} + \theta_1 a_{t-3}$$

$$Y_t = a_t - \theta_1 Y_{t-1} - \theta_1^2(Y_{t-2} + \theta_1 a_{t-3})$$
$$= a_t - \theta_1 Y_{t-1} - \theta_1^2 Y_{t-2} - \theta_1^3 a_{t-3}.$$

Continuing this substitution process indefinitely leads to the infinite series

$$Y_t = a_t - \sum_{i=1}^{\infty} \theta_1^i Y_{t-i}.$$

An ARIMA(0,0,1) process can thus be expressed identically as an autoregressive process *of infinite order*.

When the parameter θ_1 is a fraction (that is, when it satisfies the bounds of invertibility), an ARIMA(0,0,1) process has exponentially decreasing weights. To demonstrate this, let $\theta_1 = .5$. Then,

$$Y_t = a_t - \sum_{i=1}^{\infty} (.5)^i Y_{t-i}$$

$$= a_t - .5Y_{t-1} - .25Y_{t-2} - .125Y_{t-3} - \ldots - (.5)^k Y_{t-k} - \ldots.$$

But when $\theta_1 = 1.0$

$$= a_t - Y_{t-1} - Y_{t-2} - Y_{t-3} - \ldots - (1.0)^k Y_{t-k} - \ldots$$

and when $\theta_1 = 1.5$

$$= a_t - 1.5Y_{t-1} - 2.25Y_{t-2} - 3.375Y_{t-3} - \ldots$$

$$- (1.5)^k Y_{t-k} - \ldots.$$

The implications of the bounds of invertibility for moving average parameters are thus identical to the implications of the bounds of stationarity for autoregressive parameters. Unless the parameter θ_1 is less than unity in absolute value, the process is overwhelmed by its history.

We conclude this section with an input-output diagram for the ARIMA (0,0,1) process:

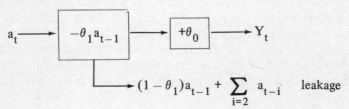

Here a random shock enters the system, is combined with a portion of the preceding random shock, has a constant, θ_0, added, and emerges from the system as the current realization, Y_t. Upon entering the system, a portion of each random shock leaks out and this behavior is typical of moving average processes. Both autoregressive and moving average processes are characterized by leakage from the ARIMA system. In ARIMA(1,0,0) processes, shocks leak out at an exponential rate. In ARIMA(0,0,1) processes, shocks leak out in quantum steps, persisting for only one observation. There is no leakage whatsoever from an ARIMA (0,d,0) model. The bounds of stationarity and invertibility permit random shocks to leak out of the ARIMA system. When these bounds are not satisfied, the ARIMA model will not mimic the characteristic behavior of autoregressive or moving average processes.

2.5 The Partial Autocorrelation Function

An ARIMA(2,0,0) process written as

$$Y_t = \phi_1 Y_{t-1} + \phi_2 Y_{t-2} + a_t$$

has a current realization determined by portions of the two preceding realizations, Y_{t-1} and Y_{t-2}, and by the current random shock, a_t. The bounds of stationarity for the parameters ϕ_1 and ϕ_2 are

$$-1 < \phi_1 < +1$$
$$\phi_1 + \phi_2 < +1$$
$$\phi_2 - \phi_1 < +1.$$

These constraints are identical to the bounds of invertibility for an ARIMA (0,0,2) process. The reader may easily demonstrate here that, when ϕ_1 and ϕ_2 are selected so as not to satisfy these bounds, a nonstationary process is implied.

The ACF of an ARIMA(0,0,2) process is expected to decay from lag to lag and this presents a real problem for model identification. If the ACF of a stationary series (or one that has been made stationary by differencing) is uniformly zero, the analyst may conclude that the series is an ARIMA (0,0,0) realization; or if the ACF has a single nonzero spike at the first lag, the analyst may conclude that the series is an ARIMA(0,0,1) realization; and spikes at ACF(1) and ACF(2) suggest an ARIMA(0,0,2) realization. If the ACF *decays* from lag to lag, however, an ARIMA(p,0,0) process in indicated. The problem, of course, is that the analyst cannot ordinarily determine the value of p from the ACF alone. In practice, both ARIMA(1,0,0) and ARIMA(2,0,0) processes have decaying ACFs which, due to stochastic variance, may have similar appearances.

A useful identification statistic in such cases is the *partial* autocorrelation function (PACF). The PACF has an interpretation not unlike that of any other measure of partial correlation. The lag-k PACF, PACF(k), is a measure of correlation between time series observation k units apart after the correlation at intermediate lags has been controlled or "partialed out." Unlike the ACF, the PACF cannot be estimated from a simple, straightforward formula. While we will not do so here, it can be demonstrated that the PACF is given by the formulae

$$PACF(1) = ACF(1)$$

$$PACF(2) = \frac{ACF(2) - [ACF(1)]^2}{1 - [ACF(1)]^2}$$

$$PACF(3) = \frac{\{ACF(3) + ACF(1)[ACF(2)]^2 + [ACF(1)]^3 - 2ACF(1)ACF(2) - [ACF(1)]^2ACF(3)\}}{1 + 2[ACF(1)]^2ACF(2) - [ACF(2)]^2 - 2[ACF(1)]^2}$$

and so forth.[8] Expressing the expected PACF in this form, the role of the PACF as a measure of partial correlation is made explicit. The PACF in fact is a "partial" (or "partialed") ACF. Expressing the PACF in this form also makes explicit the tedious arithmetic involved in its estimation. Without the proper software, the estimated PACF would be of little use to the time series analyst.

As the expected PACF is a function of the expected ACF, and as the expected ACFs of several ARIMA processes have already been derived, expected PACFs are derived by simple (but tedious) algebraic substitution. We leave these derivations to the reader and instead give the expected PACFs for several ARIMA processes as:

(1) An ARIMA(1,0,0) process whose ACF is expected to be

$$ACF(k) = \phi_1^k$$

is expected to have a nonzero PACF(1) while PACF(2) and all successive lags are expected to be zero. Specifically,

$$PACF(1) = \phi_1$$
$$PACF(2) = \ldots = PACF(k) = 0.$$

(2) An ARIMA(0,0,1) process whose ACF is expected to be

$$ACF(1) = \frac{-\theta_1}{1 + \phi_1^2}$$

$$ACF(2) = \ldots = ACF(k) = 0$$

has a decaying PACF, that is, all PACF(k) are expected to be nonzero. Specifically,

$$PACF(1) = \frac{-\theta_1}{1 + \theta_1^2}$$

$$PACF(2) = \frac{-\theta_1^2}{1 + \theta_1^2 + \theta_1^4}$$

$$PACF(3) = \frac{-\theta_1^3}{1 + \theta_1^2 + \theta_1^4 + \theta_1^6}.$$

Successive lags of the expected PACF grow smaller and smaller in absolute value. If $\theta_1 = .7$, for example,

$$PACF(1) = -.469$$
$$PACF(2) = -.283$$
$$PACF(3) = -.186$$

and so forth. In the general case, the PACF of an ARIMA(0,0,q) process is expected to decay in this manner but at a rate determined by the values of $\theta_1, \ldots, \theta_q$.

Figure 2.5 shows the expected ACFs and PACFs for several ARIMA(p,0,0) and ARIMA(p,p,q) processes. As shown, moving average processes have *decaying* PACFs while autoregressive processes have *spiking* PACFs. The ARIMA(p,0,0) process, for example, has p spikes at PACF(1), ..., PACF(p). By using both the ACF *and* the PACF then, the analyst can determine, first, whether a series is moving average or autoregressive and, second, the order of the process (the value of p or q, that is).

We have not yet derived the ACF expected of an ARIMA(2,0,0) process and, thus, cannot yet derive its expected PACF. The derivation of ACFs for higher order autoregressive processes are more complicated than the derivations of ARIMA(0,0,q) and ARIMA(1,0,0) ACFs. However, it can be demonstrated that the covariance between successive observations of an ARIMA (p,0,0) proces is[9]

$$\text{covariance}(Y_t Y_{t+k}) = \sum_{i=1}^{p} \phi_i \text{covariance}(Y_{t-i} Y_{t+k})$$

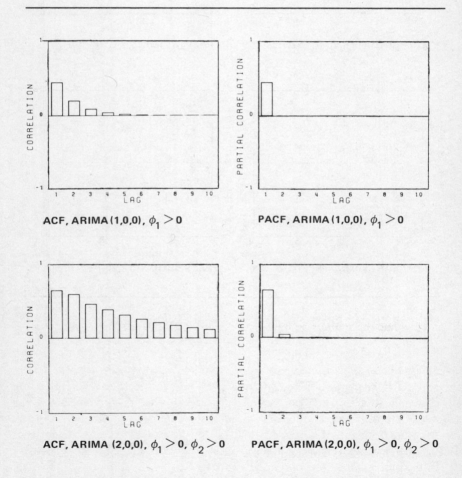

Figure 2.5   ACFs and PACFs for Several ARIMA (p,o,o) and ARIMA (o,o,q) Processes

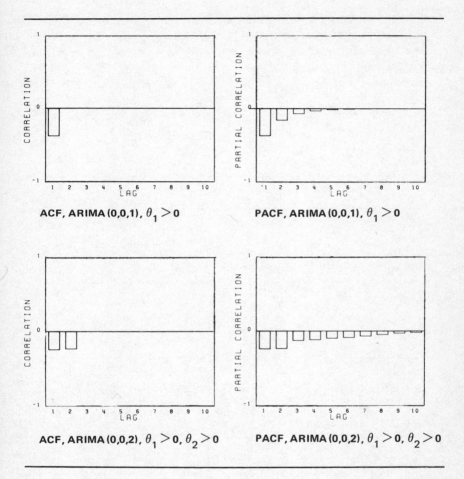

ACF, ARIMA (0,0,1), $\theta_1 > 0$

PACF, ARIMA (0,0,1), $\theta_1 > 0$

ACF, ARIMA (0,0,2), $\theta_1 > 0, \theta_2 > 0$

PACF, ARIMA (0,0,2), $\theta_1 > 0, \theta_2 > 0$

and dividing this expression by variance of the ARIMA (p,0,0) process

$$\mathrm{ACF}(k) = \sum_{i=1}^{p} \phi_i \, \mathrm{ACF}(k-i).$$

For an ARIMA(2,0,0) process, this is

$$\mathrm{ACF}(k) = \phi_1 \mathrm{ACF}(k-1) + \phi_2 \, \mathrm{ACF}(k-2).$$

With this expression, the ACF can be derived recursively. The first three lags of the ACF are expected to be

$$ACF(1) = \frac{\phi_1}{1 - \phi_2}$$

$$ACF(2) = \frac{\phi_1^2}{1 - \phi_2} + \phi_2$$

$$ACF(3) = \frac{\phi_1(\phi_2 + \phi_1^2)}{1 - \phi_2} + \phi_1 \phi_2.$$

In appearance, the ACF of an ARIMA(2,0,0) process decays, but usually at a slower rate than that of an ARIMA(1,0,0) process, as Figure 2.5 shows.

(3) Our interest is now returned to the PACF. Substituting the values of ACF(1), ACF(2), and ACF(3) into the formula, the expected PACF for an ARIMA(2,0,0) process is

$$PACF(1) = \frac{\phi_1}{1 - \phi_2}$$

$$PACF(2) = \frac{\phi_2(\phi_2 - 1)^2 - \phi_1 \phi_2}{(1 - \phi_2)^2 - \phi_1^2}$$

$$PACF(3) = 0.$$

Successive lags of the PACF for an ARIMA(2,0,0) process are all expected to be zero. In the general case, an ARIMA(p,0,0) process is expected to have nonzero values of PACF(1), . . . , PACF(p) while PACF(p+1), . . . , PACF (p+k) are all expected to be zero.

It should be clear from an examination of Figure 2.5 that the ACF and PACF are powerful identification tools. Examining these statistics, the analyst can determine whether a time series is stationary or nonstationary; whether the stationary series (or a series that has been made stationary by differencing) is white noise, moving average, or autoregressive; and the order of the moving average or autoregressive component, the integer values of q or p, that is.

2.6 Mixed Autoregressive-Moving Average Models

Our development so far has considered autoregressive and moving average structures separately. For example, when we developed the algebra of moving average models, we considered only the case of ARIMA (0,0,q) processes. Similarly, our development of autoregressive models considered only the case of ARIMA(p,0,0) processes. We will now consider *mixed* models, that is, ARIMA(p,d,q) models where both p and q are nonzero.

If our experiences are typical, only a few social science time series in a thousand will be well represented by mixed ARIMA(p,d,q) models. While mixed autoregressive-moving average processes are not logically impossible, the relationships between autoregressive and moving average processes which we have discussed place some limits on ARIMA(p,d,q) processes. These limits are ordinarily referred to as the limits of *parameter redundancy* because they take account of the fact that, in some situations, complex models are equivalent to simpler models with fewer structures.

To illustrate parameter redundancy, consider an ARIMA(1,0,1) process written as

$$Y_t = \phi_1 Y_{t-1} + a_t - \theta_1 a_{t-1}.$$

This process can be written identically as an infinite series of weighted shocks[10]

$$Y_t = a_t + (\phi_1 - \theta_1) \sum_{i=1}^{\infty} \phi_1^i a_{t-i}.$$

Written in this form, the parameter redundancy problem is explicit. First, when $\phi_1 = \theta_1$, $\phi_1 - \theta_1 = 0$, and

$$Y_t = a_t + (0) \sum_{i=1}^{\infty} \phi_1^i a_{t-i} = a_t.$$

The ARIMA(1,0,1) process reduces to an ARIMA(0,0,0) process. Similarly, when $\phi_1 = \theta_1/2$, $\phi_1 - \theta_1 = -\phi_1$, and

$$Y_t = a_t - \phi_1 \sum_{i=1}^{\infty} \phi_1^i a_{t-i} = -\phi_1 Y_{t-1} + a_t.$$

The ARIMA(1,0,1) process reduces to an ARIMA(1,0,0) process.

ARIMA(1,0,1) processes are *not* logically impossible. Both the ACF and the PACF of a mixed process are expected to decay. It happens often, however, that ARIMA(1,0,1) processes are better represented by simpler ARIMA(0,0,0), ARIMA(1,0,0), or ARIMA(0,0,1) models. Overall, the problems of parameter redundancy are so great that the analyst should not accept an ARIMA(1,0,1) model until simpler models have been ruled out.

2.7 Model Building

Having developed the algebra of ARIMA(p,d,q) models, we now address the problem of *building* an ARIMA model for a time series. Figure 2.7a shows a model-building strategy based on three procedures or steps: *identification, estimation,* and *diagnosis.* This model-building strategy is a conservative one which leads generally to an ARIMA model that is statistically adequate and yet parsimonious. As will soon be made clear, a time series model lacking these two characteristics is an arbitrary model. More specifically, unless the ARIMA model is statistically adequate and parsimonious, its application will lead to invalid inferences.

(1) *Identification* is based on the ACF and PACF estimated from the time series. The estimated ACF and PACF will indicate whether the series is stationary or nonstationary, that is, whether the series requires differencing; whether the stationary series (or one that has been made stationary through differencing) is white noise, moving average, or autoregressive; and the order of a moving average or autoregressive structure.

(2) *Estimation* requires a suitable software package. The general ARIMA(p,d,q) model is nonlinear in its parameters, so standard regression packages such as SPSS cannot be used. Most university computing centers will have an ARIMA time series package available. We discuss this issue in Section 4.0. Meanwhile, our development of the model-building strategy assumes that the reader has access to one of these computer programs.

Having identified an ARIMA(p,d,q) model for the time series, the ϕ and/or θ parameters of the model must be estimated. In this stage of the model-building procedure, the analyst must be concerned with two estimation criteria. First, parameter estimates must lie within the bounds of stationarity and/or invertibility for the autoregressive or moving average parameters. Second, parameter estimates must be statistically significant. If the parameter estimates do not satisfy both criteria, a new model must be identified.

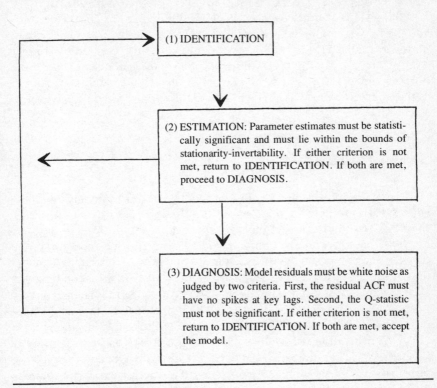

Figure 2.7a   The Model-Building Strategy

As shown in Figure 2.7a, the model-building strategy is an *iterative* strategy. Each stage of the strategy has certain absolute concerns which must be satisfied by the tentative ARIMA model. If the concerns are not satisfied, the analyst must return to the preceding stage. Suppose, for example, that the initial identification suggests an ARIMA(1,0,0) model. In the estimation stage, however, the estimate of ϕ_1 may not satisfy the bounds of stationarity; that is, the estimate of ϕ_1 may be greater than unity in absolute value. This indicates that the series is nonstationary and must be differenced. To explore this possibility, the analyst must return to the identification stage of the model-building strategy.

The statistical significance criterion is related to *parsimony*. While it may not be apparent to the reader, there are often many ARIMA(p,d,q) models which will *fit* a time series. Only one of these many models will be the most parsimonious, however. An obvious illustration of this point is that an ARIMA(1,0,0) process can be fit by an ARIMA(2,0,0) model where the parameter ϕ_2 is zero. While the ARIMA(2,0,0) model is *statistically adequate*, however, which is to say that it will *fit* the time series, it will not be the most *parsimonious* of all statistically adequate models.

(3) *Diagnosis* is concerned with the statistical adequacy of the tentative model. Having identified and satisfactorily estimated the parameters of a tentative ARIMA(p,d,q) model, the statistical adequacy of the model must be assessed. In Section 2.0, we introduced the input-output concept of ARIMA processes. Random shocks enter the ARIMA system, pass through autoregressive, integrated, and/or moving average filters, and emerge from the ARIMA system as time series observations. Model building may be conveniently thought of as the inverse procedure diagramed as

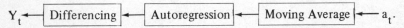

The sense of this diagram is that a time series observation is sent backward through a series of filters, emerging from the inverse ARIMA system as a random shock. The identification and estimation stages of the model-building strategy, of course, are aimed at selecting the filters which satisfy this system. *If the proper filters have been selected, if the proper ARIMA (p,d,q) model has been identified and estimated, that is, then the model residuals will not be different than white noise.*

Diagnosis consists of estimating an ACF from the model residuals. If the residuals are not different than white noise, then all lags of the residual ACF will be expected to be zero. In practice, of course, one or two lags of an ACF are expected to be statistically significant by chance alone. To test whether the *entire* residual ACF is different than that expected of a white noise process, the analyst may use the Q statistic given by the formula

$$Q(df) = N \sum_{i=1}^{k} [ACF(i)]^2 \text{ with } df = k - p - q.$$

This formula assumes an ACF of k lags estimated from N residuals. The Q statistic is distributed as a chi-square with degrees of freedom determined by the length of the ACF and the number of autoregressive and/or moving average parameters in the model. For example, an ACF of 30 lags estimated from the residuals of an ARIMA(0,0,1) model has 29 degrees of freedom. A null hypothesis that the model residuals are white noise is

$$H_0: a_t \sim NID(0, \sigma^2).$$

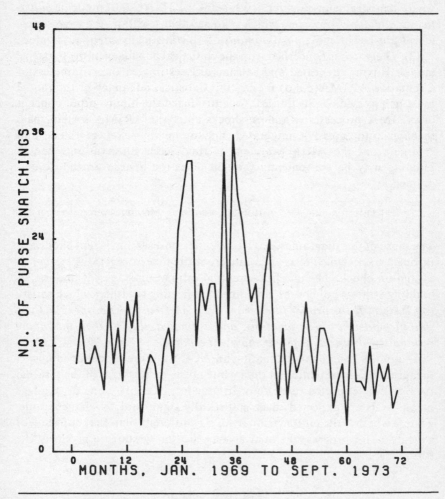

Figure 2.7b Hyde Park Purse Snatchings Time Series

This null hypothesis may be expressed in terms of the Q statistic as

$$H_0: Q = 0.$$

If the Q statistic is significant at a nominal level (say .05), then these null hypotheses are rejected. The analyst concludes that the tentative ARIMA model is statistically inadequate; its residuals are different than white noise. If the Q statistic is *not* significant, however, the null hypothesis is accepted. The analyst concludes that the model residuals are not different than white noise and the tentative model is accepted.

We will now illustrate the model-building strategy with an example analysis. Figure 2.7b shows a time series of purse snatchings reported to the police in the Hyde Park neighborhood of Chicago. The first observation of this series is the total number of purse snatchings for the first 28 days (four weeks) of 1969; the second observation is the total for the second 28 days; the 71st observation is the total for the sixth 28-day period of 1974. This method of reporting insures that there are an equal number of days in each reporting period. Our analysis will, of course, follow the strategy outlined in Figure 2.7a.

(1) *Identification.* As a first step, an ACF and PACF are estimated from the raw data. These statistics, shown in Figure 2.7c, indicate that the series is the realization of a *stationary* process; the series will not have to be differenced. The key to this identification is in the ACF which dies out much too quickly. Moreover, a moving average process is not indicated by this ACF. A moving average process would be indicated by one or two salient spikes in the ACF. Instead, the ACF exhibits a rough pattern of decay, indicating an autoregressive process and, hence, an ARIMA(p,0,0) model for this time series. The PACF has two statistically significant spikes at PACF(1) and PACF(2) which suggest an ARIMA(2,0,0) model. This is written as

$$Y_t = \phi_1 Y_{t-1} + \phi_2 Y_{t-2} + a_t.$$

There are two parameters to be estimated in this model.

(2) *Estimation.* For an ARIMA(2,0,0) model, parameter estimates are

$$\hat{\phi}_1 = .31 \text{ with t statistic} = 2.67.$$

$$\hat{\phi}_2 = .40 \text{ with t statistic} = 3.45.$$

Both parameter estimates are statistically significant at a .05 level or better; also, the estimates satisfy the bounds of stationarity for autoregressive parameters.

(3) *Diagnosis.* As a final step of the model-building procedure, the residuals of the tentative model must not be different than white noise. An ACF estimated for the residuals, shown in Figure 2.7d, has no statistically significant spikes at the low-order lags. The Q statistic for this diagnostic ACF is 17.8, a value of Q which, for 22 degrees of freedom, is statistically significant only at the .71 level. To reject the null hypothesis that these residuals are white noise, of course, we require a value of Q to

52

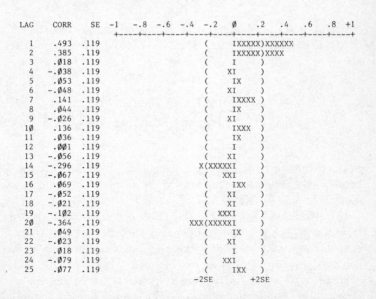

```
SERIES. . HPPS  (NOBS=  71)   HYDE PARK PURSE SNATCHINGS
NO. OF VALID OBSERVATIONS  =   71.

AUTOCORRELATIONS OF LAGS 1 - 25.
Q( 25, 71) = 110.68     SIC =       .000


   LAG   CORR   SE  -1  -.8  -.6  -.4  -.2   0   .2   .4   .6   .8  +1
                    +----+----+----+----+----+----+----+----+----+----+
     1   .439  .119                          (   IXXXXX)XXXXXX
     2   .534  .145                          (   IXXXXX)XXXXXX
     3   .363  .170                        (   IXXXXXXXX*
     4   .294  .181                        (   IXXXXXXX )
     5   .261  .187                        (   IXXXXXXX )
     6   .163  .192                      (   IXXXX     )
     7   .243  .194                      (   IXXXXXX   )
     8   .183  .199                      (   IXXXXX    )
     9   .179  .201                      (   IXXXX     )
    10   .243  .203                      (   IXXXXXX   )
    11   .204  .207                      (   IXXXXX    )
    12   .227  .210                      (   IXXXXXX   )
    13   .147  .214                      (   IXXXX     )
    14  -.022  .215                      (    XI       )
    15  -.023  .215                      (    XI       )
    16  -.076  .215                      (   XXI       )
    17  -.092  .215                      (   XXI       )
    18  -.098  .216                      (   XXI       )
    19  -.147  .217                      (   XXXXI     )
    20  -.277  .218                      (  XXXXXXXI   )
    21  -.219  .223                      (   XXXXXI    )
    22  -.286  .226                      (  XXXXXXXI   )
    23  -.196  .231                    (   XXXXXI       )
    24  -.305  .233                    (  XXXXXXXXI     )
    25  -.186  .239                    (   XXXXXI       )
                                    -2SE            +2SE


PARTIAL AUTOCORRELATIONS OF LAGS 1 - 25.


   LAG   CORR   SE  -1  -.8  -.6  -.4  -.2   0   .2   .4   .6   .8  +1
                    +----+----+----+----+----+----+----+----+----+----+
     1   .493  .119                          (   IXXXXX)XXXXXX
     2   .385  .119                          (   IXXXXX)XXXX
     3   .018  .119                          (    I     )
     4  -.038  .119                          (   XI     )
     5   .053  .119                          (   IX     )
     6  -.048  .119                          (   XI     )
     7   .141  .119                          (   IXXXX  )
     8   .044  .119                          (   IX     )
     9  -.026  .119                          (   XI     )
    10   .136  .119                          (   IXXX   )
    11   .036  .119                          (   IX     )
    12   .001  .119                          (   I      )
    13  -.056  .119                          (   XI     )
    14  -.296  .119                      X (XXXXXI     )
    15  -.067  .119                          (  XXI     )
    16   .069  .119                          (   IXX    )
    17  -.052  .119                          (   XI     )
    18  -.021  .119                          (   XI     )
    19  -.102  .119                        (  XXXI      )
    20  -.364  .119                      XXX(XXXXXI     )
    21   .049  .119                          (   IX     )
    22  -.023  .119                          (   XI     )
    23   .018  .119                          (   I      )
    24  -.079  .119                          (  XXI     )
    25   .077  .119                          (   IXX    )
                                        -2SE            +2SE
```

Figure 2.7c ACF and PACF for the Raw Hyde Park Series

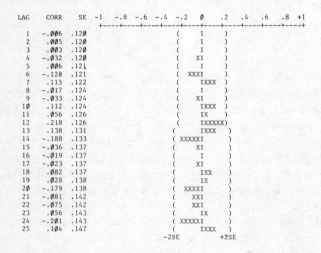

```
SERIES. . RESIDUAL  (NOBS=  71)  HYDE PARK PURSE SNATCHING RESIDUALS
NO. OF VALID OBSERVATIONS  =      69.

AUTOCORRELATIONS OF LAGS 1 - 25.
Q( 22,  69) = 17.814     SIG =      .717


 LAG   CORR    SE  -1  -.8  -.6  -.4  -.2   Ø   .2   .4   .6   .8  +1
                    +----+----+----+----+----+----+----+----+----+----+
   1  -.ØØ6  .12Ø                       (      I      )
   2   .ØØ5  .12Ø                       (      I      )
   3   .ØØ3  .12Ø                       (      I      )
   4  -.Ø32  .12Ø                       (     XI      )
   5   .ØØ6  .121                       (      I      )
   6  -.128  .121                       (    XXXI     )
   7   .115  .122                       (      IXXX   )
   8  -.Ø17  .124                       (      I      )
   9  -.Ø33  .124                       (     XI      )
  1Ø   .112  .124                       (      IXXX   )
  11   .Ø56  .126                       (      IX     )
  12   .218  .126                       (      IXXXXX)
  13   .138  .131                     (      IXXX     )
  14  -.188  .133                     ( XXXXXI        )
  15  -.Ø36  .137                     (     XI        )
  16  -.Ø19  .137                     (      I        )
  17  -.Ø23  .137                     (     XI        )
  18   .Ø82  .137                     (      IXX      )
  19   .Ø28  .138                     (      IX       )
  2Ø  -.179  .138                     (  XXXXI        )
  21  -.Ø81  .142                     (    XXI        )
  22  -.Ø75  .142                     (    XXI        )
  23   .Ø56  .143                     (      IX       )
  24  -.2Ø1  .143                     ( XXXXXXI       )
  25   .1Ø4  .147                     (      IXXX     )
                                      -2SE        +2SE
```

PARTIAL AUTOCORRELATIONS OF LAGS 1 - 25.

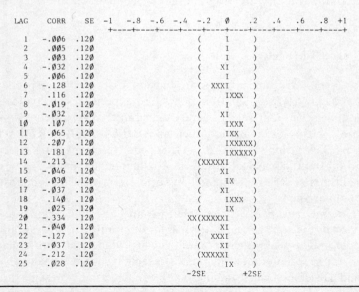

```
 LAG   CORR    SE  -1  -.8  -.6  -.4  -.2   Ø   .2   .4   .6   .8  +1
                    +----+----+----+----+----+----+----+----+----+----+
   1  -.ØØ6  .12Ø                       (      I      )
   2   .ØØ5  .12Ø                       (      I      )
   3   .ØØ3  .12Ø                       (      I      )
   4  -.Ø32  .12Ø                       (     XI      )
   5   .ØØ6  .12Ø                       (      I      )
   6  -.128  .12Ø                       (    XXXI     )
   7   .116  .12Ø                       (      IXXX   )
   8  -.Ø19  .12Ø                       (      I      )
   9  -.Ø32  .12Ø                       (     XI      )
  1Ø   .1Ø7  .12Ø                       (      IXXX   )
  11   .Ø65  .12Ø                       (      IXX    )
  12   .2Ø7  .12Ø                       (      IXXXXX)
  13   .181  .12Ø                       (      IXXXXX)
  14  -.213  .12Ø                     (XXXXXXI        )
  15  -.Ø46  .12Ø                       (     XI      )
  16   .Ø3Ø  .12Ø                       (      IX     )
  17  -.Ø37  .12Ø                       (     XI      )
  18   .14Ø  .12Ø                       (      IXXX   )
  19   .Ø25  .12Ø                       (      IX     )
  2Ø  -.334  .12Ø                    XX(XXXXXI        )
  21  -.Ø4Ø  .12Ø                       (     XI      )
  22  -.127  .12Ø                       (    XXXI     )
  23  -.Ø37  .12Ø                       (     XI      )
  24  -.212  .12Ø                     (XXXXXXI        )
  25   .Ø28  .12Ø                       (      IX     )
                                      -2SE        +2SE
```

Figure 2.7d   ACF for the Hyde Park Model Residuals

be statistically significant at the .05 level or better. Because the residual ACF has no statistically significant low-order spikes, and because its Q statistic is insignificant, we must conclude that these residuals are not different than white noise. The tentative model must be accepted.

The ARIMA(2,0,0) model for the Hyde Park purse snatching time series is

$$Y_t = .31Y_{t-1} + .40Y_{t-2} + a_t.$$

This model was identified empirically, its parameters estimated and tested, and its residuals diagnosed. Of course, if the logical tests in the estimation stage (parameter estimates must be statistically significant and must satisfy the bounds of stationarity) or in the diagnosis stage (the model residuals must not be different than white noise) had indicated a problem, we would have returned to the identification stage. A new model would have been identified, its parameters estimated, and its residuals diagnosed. The procedure would have continued iteratively until a statistically adequate model was built.

Once built, the model for this time series can be used for impact assessment. In the 42nd time period of this series, a community whistle-alert program was instituted. At a later point, we will return to this time series to determine whether the program had any impact on the level of purse snatchings in Hyde Park.

2.8 Seasonal Models

The Hyde Park time series is an unusual series in two respects. First, it requires an ARIMA(2,0,0) model. If our experiences are typical, most of the time series that social scientists encounter will be well represented by zero- or first-order models such as ARIMA(0,0,0), ARIMA(1,0,0), ARIMA(0,0,1), and ARIMA(0,1,1). Second, the Hyde Park time series has no substantial seasonal variation. Again, if our experiences are typical, most of the time series encountered by social scientists will have substantial seasonal variance.

We define *seasonality* (or seasonal variance) as any periodic or cyclic behavior in the time series. A time series of monthly traffic fatalities, for example, might peak in winter months when road conditions are at their worst; a time series of monthly retail sales might similarly peak in November and December when families shop for Christmas presents; and any time series composed of aggregated events is likely to be seasonal simply because some months are longer than others. Knowing nothing else about a time series except that it has a strong seasonal component, the analyst can make predictions about the series. Predictability here is due to seasonal variance which must be controlled or modeled.

There are many approaches to time series analysis including the better known regression approach (Ostrom, 1978). The ARIMA approach has many advantages over these alternative approaches, however. In the case of seasonality, for example, alternative approaches often require a "seasonal adjustment" or "deseasonalization" of the time series prior to analysis. The ARIMA approach, in contrast, *models* the dependencies which define seasonality.

To illustrate just how seasonality may be modeled, we write out an N-month time series as

JAN	FEB	MAR	APR	MAY	JUN	JUL	AUG	SEP	OCT	NOV	DEC
Y_1	Y_2	Y_3	Y_4	Y_5	Y_6	Y_7	Y_8	Y_9	Y_{10}	Y_{11}	Y_{12}
Y_{13}	Y_{14}	Y_{15}	Y_{16}	Y_{17}	Y_{18}	Y_{19}	Y_{20}	Y_{21}	Y_{22}	Y_{23}	Y_{24}

Y_{N-11} ...   ... Y_N

An ARIMA(p,d,q) model describes relationships among adjacent observations of this series. An ARIMA(1,0,0) model, for example, uses the preceding observation to predict the current observation. An ARIMA (0,0,1) model, on the other hand, uses the preceding shock (which is part of the preceding observation) to predict the current observation. If a time series is seasonal, however, there will be analogous relationships between Y_1 (or January of the first year) and Y_{13} (Jaunary of the second year). As one might suspect, there are *seasonal* autoregressive, integrated, and moving average structures whose orders are denoted by P, D, and Q, respectively. More specifically:

(1) *Seasonal nonstationarity.* A process may drift or trend in annual steps or increments. Agricultural production time series tend to exhibit nonstationarity of this sort due, presumably, to the prominence of the growing season in these processes. To account for seasonal nonstationarity, the time series must be differenced seasonally. That is,

$$Y_t - Y_{t-12} = \theta_0$$

for monthly data. A process well represented by this model would trend or drift in annual steps such as

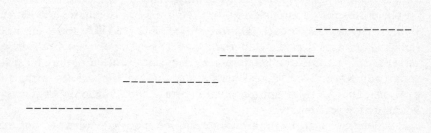

rather than as month-to-month steps.

(2) *Seasonal autoregression*. The current observation of the time series may depend upon the corresponding observation of the series from the preceding year. That is, for monthly data

$$Y_t = \phi_{12} Y_{t-12} + a_t.$$

Our comments on higher order ARIMA(p,0,0) and ARIMA(0,0,q) models apply to ARIMA(P,0,0) and ARIMA(0,0,Q) models as well. While a second-order seasonal autoregressive process is possible, it would be a rare find.

(3) *Seasonal moving averages*. The current observation of the time series may depend upon the random shock from the preceding year. That is,

$$Y_t = a_t - \theta_{12} a_{t-12}.$$

And of course, the seasonal structure may be composed of any combination of these structures.

As one might suspect, the identification of a seasonal ARIMA structure proceeds from an examination of the ACF and PACF. In fact, the expected ACF and PACF of an ARIMA(P,D,Q) process and the expected ACF and PACF of the analogous ARIMA(p,d,q) process are identical. The difference is that, for the seasonal process, patterns of spiking and decay appear at the *seasonal* lags of the ACF and PACF. Assuming monthly data, the seasonal lags are ACF(12), . . . , ACF(12k).

Thus

(1) Seasonal nonstationarity is indicated by an ACF that dies out slowly from seasonal lag to seasonal lag. In other words

$$ACF(12) \approx ACF(24) \approx ACF(36) \approx \ldots \approx ACF(12k).$$

If a time series requires seasonal differencing, even ACF(60) will sometimes be nonzero.

(2) Seasonal autoregression is indicated by an ACF that dies out exponentially from seasonal lag to seasonal lag.

$$ACF(12) \quad = \phi_{12}$$

$$ACF(24) \quad = \phi_{12}^2$$

$$ACF(12k) = \phi_{12}^k.$$

The PACF of an ARIMA(P,0,0) process will have spikes at PACF(12), . . ., PACF(12P). In practice, of course, P = 1 in almost all cases.

(3) Seasonal moving averages are indicated by an ACF with spikes at ACF(12), . . . , ACF(12Q). Again, however, Q = 1 in almost all cases.

Most time series processes with seasonal ARIMA behavior will exhibit regular ARIMA behavior as well. It might seem reasonable to incorporate regular and seasonal structures additively. For example, a process with both regular and seasonal autoregressive structures might be written as

$$Y_t = \phi_1 Y_{t-1} + \phi_{12} Y_{t-12} + a_t.$$

Here the regular and seasonal structures are merely added together and, hence, the model is *additive*. A more powerful model can be realized by incorporating regular and seasonal structures *multiplicatively*, however. Such a model would be written as

$$Y_t = \phi_1 Y_{t-1} + \phi_{12} Y_{t-12} - \phi_1 \phi_{12} Y_{t-13} + a_t.$$

The only difference between additive and multiplicative models in this case is the $\phi_1 \phi_{12} Y_{t-13}$ term. Put simply, the multiplicative model gives weight to the dependence between the seasonally lagged observation (Y_{t-12}) and the preceding observation (Y_{t-13}). The multiplicative scheme will ordinarily give a better representation of seasonality for the obvious reason that it uses an extra piece of information (Y_{t-13}). When ϕ_1 and ϕ_{12} are both small, of course, their product, $\phi_1 \phi_{12}$, will be nearly zero and the multiplicative and additive forms of the model will be approximately identical.

The general seasonal model is denoted ARIMA(p,d,q)(P,D,Q)s which makes its multiplicative nature explicit. The subscripted parameter S denotes the length of the period or cycle. For monthly data, that is, S = 12; but for quarterly data, S = 4; and for weekly data, S = 52.

Students of time series analysis are often intimidated by the sudden jump from nonseasonal to seasonal models. This anxiety is unfounded. If the principles of nonseasonal ARIMA(p,d,q) models are well understood, seasonal ARIMA(p,d,q)(P,D,Q)s models and modeling procedures can be learned with a little extra effort. To demonstrate this, we will now build an ARIMA(p,d,q)(P,D,Q)s model for the Sutter County Workforce time series which we introduced earlier. Eyeballing this plotted series (Figure 1b), the reader should immediately notice that the series spikes every 12 months, indicating a substantial seasonal component. The series also appears to trend upward, indicating a nonstationary process. These eyeball impressions will be confirmed by the analysis.

(1) *Identification.* Figure 2.8a shows the ACF and PACF of the raw or undifferenced time series. Nonstationarity is obviously indicated, so the series must be differenced. Figure 2.8b shows the ACF and PACF estimated from the *regularly* differenced series. Seasonal nonstationarity is indicated. The key to this identification are the large values of ACF(12) and ACF(24). ACF(36), ACF(48), and ACF(60), not shown here, are also quite large. The series must now be differenced seasonally as well. Regular differencing amounts to subtracting the first observation from the second, the second from the third, and so forth. That is,

$$Z_t = Y_t - Y_{t-1}$$

where the tth observation of the regularly differenced series is denoted by Z_t. The Z_t series is then seasonally differenced.

$$W_t = Z_t - Z_{t-12}$$
$$= (Y_t - Y_{t-1}) - (Y_{t-12} - Y_{t-13})$$

where the tth observation of the regularly *and* seasonally differenced series is denoted by W_t. It is important to understand that the series could be seasonally differenced first

$$Z_t = Y_t - Y_{t-12}$$

```
SERIES.. EMPLOY   (NOBS= 252)  SUTTER COUNTY EMPLOYMENT, 1/45 TO 12/66
NO. OF VALID OBSERVATIONS  =   252.

AUTOCORRELATIONS OF LAGS 1 - 30.
Q( 30, 252) =  2277.8     SIG =    0.000

   LAG   CORR    SE  -1  -.8  -.6  -.4  -.2   0   .2   .4   .6   .8  +1
                      +----+----+----+----+----+----+----+----+----+----+
     1   .874   .063                           (  IXX)XXXXXXXXXXXXXXXXXXX
     2   .757   .100                         (  IXXXX)XXXXXXXXXXXXXX
     3   .664   .121                        (  IXXXXX)XXXXXXXXXX
     4   .585   .134                       (  IXXXXXX)XXXXXXXX
     5   .514   .144                      (  IXXXXXX)XXXXXX
     6   .484   .151                     (  IXXXXXX)XXXX
     7   .490   .157                     (  IXXXXXX)XXXX
     8   .534   .163                     (  IXXXXXX)XXXXX
     9   .580   .170                    (  IXXXXXXX)XXXXX
    10   .633   .178                    (  IXXXXXXX)XXXXXXX
    11   .722   .186                    (  IXXXXXXX)XXXXXXXXX
    12   .792   .197                   (  IXXXXXXXX)XXXXXXXXXX
    13   .700   .209                   (  IXXXXXXXX)XXXXXXX
    14   .595   .219                  (  IXXXXXXXXX)XXXX
    15   .512   .225                  (  IXXXXXXXXX)XX
    16   .432   .229                  (  IXXXXXXXXX*
    17   .368   .233                  (  IXXXXXXXX  )
    18   .341   .235                  (  IXXXXXXXX  )
    19   .347   .237                  (  IXXXXXXXX  )
    20   .392   .239                  (  IXXXXXXXX  )
    21   .444   .241                  (  IXXXXXXXXX)
    22   .499   .245                  (  IXXXXXXXXX*
    23   .578   .249                  (  IXXXXXXXXX)XX
    24   .653   .254                 (  IXXXXXXXXXX)XXX
    25   .578   .261                 (  IXXXXXXXXXX)X
    26   .486   .266                 (  IXXXXXXXXXX)
    27   .405   .269                 (  IXXXXXXXXX  )
    28   .333   .272                (  IXXXXXXXX   )
    29   .278   .273                (  IXXXXXXX    )
    30   .249   .274                (  IXXXXXX     )
                                   -2SE               +2SE


PARTIAL AUTOCORRELATIONS OF LAGS 1 - 30.

   LAG   CORR    SE  -1  -.8  -.6  -.4  -.2   0   .2   .4   .6   .8  +1
                      +----+----+----+----+----+----+----+----+----+----+
     1   .874   .063                         (  IXX)XXXXXXXXXXXXXXXXXXX
     2  -.027   .063                         ( XI  )
     3   .038   .063                         (  IX )
     4   .007   .063                         (  I  )
     5  -.008   .063                         (  I  )
     6   .142   .063                         (  IXX)X
     7   .149   .063                         (  IXX)X
     8   .217   .063                         (  IXX)XX
     9   .114   .063                         (  IXX*
    10   .165   .063                         (  IXX)X
    11   .336   .063                         (  IXX)XXXXX
    12   .224   .063                         (  IXX)XXX
    13  -.512   .063            XXXXXXXXXXX(XXI  )
    14  -.163   .063                    X (XXI  )
    15  -.005   .063                         (  I  )
    16  -.047   .063                         ( XI  )
    17   .024   .063                         (  IX )
    18   .003   .063                         (  I  )
    19  -.004   .063                         (  I  )
    20   .062   .063                         (  IXX)
    21   .106   .063                         (  IXX*
    22   .052   .063                         (  IX )
    23  -.009   .063                         (  I  )
    24   .200   .063                         (  IXX)XX
    25  -.182   .063                     XX (XXI  )
    26  -.072   .063                        (XXI  )
    27  -.018   .063                         (  I  )
    28   .012   .063                         (  I  )
    29   .022   .063                         (  IX )
    30  -.050   .063                         ( XI  )
                                             -2SE +2SE
```

Figure 2.8a   ACF and PACF for the Raw Sutter County Series

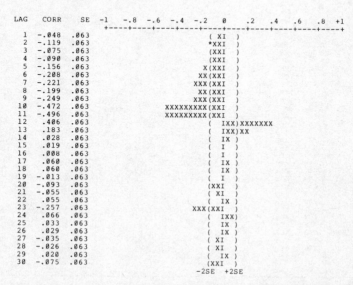

```
SERIES.. EMPLOY   (NOBS= 252)  SUTTER COUNTY EMPLOYMENT, 1/45 TO 12/66
DIFFERENCED  1 TIME(S) OF ORDER  1.
NO. OF VALID OBSERVATIONS  =   251.

AUTOCORRELATIONS OF LAGS 1 - 30.
Q( 30, 251) = 296.02      SIG =    0.000


   LAG   CORR    SE  -1   -.8  -.6  -.4  -.2   0    .2   .4   .6   .8  +1
                      +----+----+----+----+----+----+----+----+----+----+
     1  -.046   .063                          ( XI  )
     2  -.116   .063                         *XXI  )
     3  -.062   .064                          (XXI  )
     4  -.066   .064                          (XXI  )
     5  -.124   .065                         *XXI  )
     6  -.151   .066                        X(XXI  )
     7  -.116   .067                         *XXI  )
     8  -.041   .068                          ( XI  )
     9  -.043   .068                          ( XI  )
    10  -.157   .068                        X(XXI  )
    11   .080   .069                          (  IXX )
    12   .713   .070                          (  IXX)XXXXXXXXXXXXXXX
    13   .045   .094                          (  IX  )
    14  -.096   .095                          ( XXI  )
    15  -.051   .095                          (  XI  )
    16  -.074   .095                          (  XXI )
    17  -.101   .095                          ( XXXI )
    18  -.144   .096                          (XXXXI )
    19  -.127   .097                          ( XXXI )
    20  -.049   .097                          (  XI  )
    21  -.032   .097                          (  XI  )
    22  -.111   .097                          ( XXXI )
    23   .021   .098                          (  IX  )
    24   .651   .098                          (  IXXX)XXXXXXXXXXX
    25   .074   .114                          (  IXX )
    26  -.057   .114                          (  XI  )
    27  -.072   .114                          (  XXI )
    28  -.069   .114                          (  XXI )
    29  -.077   .114                          (  XXI )
    30  -.171   .115                          ( XXXXI )
                                           -2SE       +2SE


PARTIAL AUTOCORRELATIONS OF LAGS 1 - 30.


   LAG   CORR    SE  -1   -.8  -.6  -.4  -.2   0    .2   .4   .6   .8  +1
                      +----+----+----+----+----+----+----+----+----+----+
     1  -.048   .063                          ( XI  )
     2  -.119   .063                         *XXI  )
     3  -.075   .063                          (XXI  )
     4  -.090   .063                          (XXI  )
     5  -.156   .063                        X(XXI  )
     6  -.208   .063                       XX(XXI  )
     7  -.221   .063                      XXX(XXI  )
     8  -.199   .063                       XX(XXI  )
     9  -.249   .063                      XXX(XXI  )
    10  -.472   .063                XXXXXXXXX(XXI  )
    11  -.496   .063                XXXXXXXXX(XXI  )
    12   .406   .063                          (  IXX)XXXXXXX
    13   .183   .063                          (  IXX)XX
    14   .028   .063                          (  IX  )
    15   .019   .063                          (  I   )
    16   .008   .063                          (  I   )
    17   .060   .063                          (  IX  )
    18   .060   .063                          (  IX  )
    19  -.013   .063                          (  I   )
    20  -.093   .063                          (XXI  )
    21  -.055   .063                          ( XI  )
    22   .055   .063                          (  IX  )
    23  -.257   .063                       XXX(XXI  )
    24   .066   .063                          (  IXX)
    25   .033   .063                          (  IX  )
    26   .029   .063                          (  IX  )
    27  -.035   .063                          ( XI  )
    28  -.026   .063                          ( XI  )
    29   .020   .063                          (  IX  )
    30  -.075   .063                          (XXI  )
                                           -2SE  +2SE
```

Figure 2.8b   ACF and PACF for the Regularly Differenced Sutter County Series

```
SERIES.. EMPLOY   (NOBS= 252)  SUTTER COUNTY EMPLOYMENT, 1/45 TO 12/66
DIFFERENCED  1 TIME(S) OF ORDER  1.
DIFFERENCED  1 TIME(S) OF ORDER 12.
NO. OF VALID OBSERVATIONS  =   239.

AUTOCORRELATIONS OF LAGS 1 - 30.
Q( 30, 239) =  151.93      SIG =    .000


   LAG   CORR    SE  -1  -.8  -.6  -.4  -.2   0    .2   .4   .6   .8  +1
                       +----+----+----+----+----+----+----+----+----+----+
    1   -.430  .065              XXXXXXX(XXI  )
    2    .065  .076                       (  IXX  )
    3   -.076  .076                       ( XXI    )
    4    .002  .076                       (  I    )
    5   -.056  .076                       ( XI    )
    6    .014  .076                       (  I    )
    7    .049  .076                       (  IX   )
    8    .039  .077                       (  IX   )
    9    .040  .077                       (  IX   )
   10   -.144  .077                      *XXXI    )
   11    .306  .078                       (  IXXX)XXXX
   12   -.439  .083              XXXXXXX(XXXI    )
   13    .120  .092                       (  IXXX )
   14   -.037  .093                       ( XI    )
   15    .066  .093                       (  IXX  )
   16   -.045  .093                       ( XI    )
   17    .025  .093                       (  IX   )
   18    .058  .093                       (  IX   )
   19   -.105  .093                       ( XXXI  )
   20    .030  .094                       (  IX   )
   21   -.021  .094                       ( XI    )
   22    .088  .094                       (  IXX  )
   23   -.150  .094                       (XXXXI  )
   24    .049  .095                       (  IX   )
   25    .001  .095                       (  I    )
   26    .131  .095                       (  IXXX )
   27   -.132  .096                       ( XXXI  )
   28    .030  .097                       (  IX   )
   29    .060  .097                       (  IXX  )
   30   -.123  .097                       ( XXXI   )
                                           -2SE    +2SE

PARTIAL AUTOCORRELATIONS OF LAGS 1 - 30.


   LAG   CORR    SE  -1  -.8  -.6  -.4  -.2   0    .2   .4   .6   .8  +1
                       +----+----+----+----+----+----+----+----+----+----+
    1   -.430  .065              XXXXXXX(XXI  )
    2   -.147  .065                     X(XXI  )
    3   -.135  .065                      *XXI   )
    4   -.103  .065                      *XXI   )
    5   -.136  .065                      *XXI   )
    6   -.104  .065                      *XXI   )
    7   -.007  .065                       (  I  )
    8    .061  .065                       (  IXX )
    9    .115  .065                       (  IXX*
   10   -.081  .065                      (XXI   )
   11    .300  .065                       (  IXX)XXXXX
   12   -.230  .065                    XXX(XXI  )
   13   -.191  .065                     XX(XXI  )
   14   -.134  .065                      *XXI   )
   15   -.090  .065                      (XXI   )
   16   -.119  .065                      *XXI   )
   17   -.129  .065                      *XXI   )
   18    .008  .065                       (  I  )
   19   -.103  .065                      *XXI   )
   20   -.011  .065                       (  I  )
   21    .082  .065                       (  IXX)
   22    .029  .065                       (  IX )
   23    .062  .065                       (  IXX)
   24   -.162  .065                     X(XXI   )
   25   -.141  .065                     X(XXI   )
   26    .040  .065                       (  IX )
   27   -.093  .065                       (XXI  )
   28   -.129  .065                      *XXI   )
   29   -.041  .065                       ( XI  )
   30   -.074  .065                       (XXI  )
                                           -2SE  +2SE
```

Figure 2.8c ACF and PACF for the Regularly and Seasonally Differenced Sutter County Series

and then regularly differenced

$$W_t = Z_t - Z_{t-1}$$
$$= (Y_t - Y_{t-12}) - (Y_{t-1} - Y_{t-13})$$

with the same result. Figure 2.8c shows the ACF and PACF estimated from the regularly *and* seasonally differenced time series. Spikes at ACF(1) and ACF(12) indicate the presence of regular and seasonal moving averages. This suggests an ARIMA$(0,1,1)(0,1,1)_{12}$ model for the time series which may be written as

$$W_t = \theta_0 + a_t - \theta_1 a_{t-1} - \theta_{12} a_{t-12} + \theta_1 \theta_{12} a_{t-13}.$$

In fact, there is little ambiguity in this identification.

(2) *Estimation*. The parameter estimates for this tenative model are

$$\hat{\theta}_0 = -.52 \quad \text{with t statistic} = -.22$$
$$\hat{\theta}_1 = .60 \quad \text{with t statistic} = 11.38$$
$$\hat{\theta}_{12} = .68 \quad \text{with t statistic} = 13.33.$$

The estimate of θ_0 is not statistically significant, so this parameter must be dropped from the model. Because the ARIMA$(0,1,1)(0,1,1)_{12}$ model posits a nonstationary process, θ_0 is interpreted as the *slope* or *trend* of the process. In this case, the statistically insignificant estimate is interpreted to mean that the series is *drifting* or, more precisely, that the movement of this process is not significantly different than drift. The estimates of θ_1 and θ_{12} are both statistically significant and otherwise acceptable. Both lie within the bounds of invertibility.

(3) *Diagnosis*. Figure 2.8d shows the ACF and PACF estimated from the model residuals. There are no significant spikes at the early or seasonal lags. More important, the Q statistic for this ACF is not significant at a .05 level. The residuals of this model are not different than white noise, so the model is accepted.

```
SERIES.. RESIDUAL (NOBS= 239)  SUTTER COUNTY EMPLOYMENT RESIDUALS
NO. OF VALID OBSERVATIONS  =    239.

AUTOCORRELATIONS OF LAGS 1 - 30.
Q( 28, 239) =  28.304      SIG =     .448


  LAG   CORR    SE  -1  -.8  -.6  -.4  -.2    0   .2   .4   .6   .8  +1
                    +----+----+----+----+----+----+----+----+----+----+
    1   .050   .065                          (   IX )
    2  -.016   .065                          (   I  )
    3  -.112   .065                         *XXI  )
    4  -.054   .066                          ( XI  )
    5  -.024   .066                          ( XI  )
    6   .077   .066                          (  IXX)
    7   .080   .066                          (  IXX)
    8   .087   .067                          (  IXX)
    9  -.025   .067                          ( XI  )
   10  -.127   .067                         *XXI  )
   11   .037   .068                          (  IX )
   12  -.009   .068                          (  I  )
   13  -.034   .068                          ( XI  )
   14  -.031   .068                          ( XI  )
   15  -.065   .068                          (XXI  )
   16  -.061   .069                          (XXI  )
   17   .025   .069                          (  IX )
   18   .034   .069                          (  IX )
   19  -.033   .069                          ( XI  )
   20   .008   .069                          (  I  )
   21  -.020   .069                          ( XI  )
   22  -.034   .069                          ( XI  )
   23  -.113   .069                         *XXI  )
   24   .017   .070                          (  I  )
   25   .123   .070                          (  IXX*
   26   .098   .071                          (  IXX )
   27  -.072   .071                          ( XXI  )
   28  -.024   .072                          ( XI  )
   29   .037   .072                          (  IX )
   30  -.043   .072                          ( XI  )
                                             -2SE    +2SE

PARTIAL AUTOCORRELATIONS OF LAGS 1 - 30.


  LAG   CORR    SE  -1  -.8  -.6  -.4  -.2    0   .2   .4   .6   .8  +1
                    +----+----+----+----+----+----+----+----+----+----+
    1   .050   .065                          (  IX )
    2  -.018   .065                          (  I  )
    3  -.111   .065                         *XXI  )
    4  -.044   .065                          ( XI  )
    5  -.023   .065                          ( XI  )
    6   .067   .065                          (  IXX)
    7   .064   .065                          (  IXX)
    8   .078   .065                          (  IXX)
    9  -.017   .065                          (  I  )
   10  -.106   .065                         *XXI  )
   11   .074   .065                          (  IXX)
   12  -.016   .065                          (  I  )
   13  -.065   .065                          (XXI  )
   14  -.044   .065                          ( XI  )
   15  -.078   .065                          (XXI  )
   16  -.056   .065                          ( XI  )
   17   .029   .065                          (  IX )
   18   .029   .065                          (  IX )
   19  -.062   .065                          (XXI  )
   20   .013   .065                          (  I  )
   21   .021   .065                          (  IX )
   22  -.025   .065                          ( XI  )
   23  -.113   .065                         *XXI  )
   24   .021   .065                          (  IX )
   25   .104   .065                          (  IXX*
   26   .060   .065                          (  IXX)
   27  -.074   .065                          (XXI  )
   28  -.007   .065                          (  I  )
   29   .064   .065                          (  IXX)
   30  -.032   .065                          ( XI  )
                                             -2SE   +2SE
```

Figure 2.8d   ACF for the Sutter County Model Residuals

The $ARIMA(0,1,1)(0,1,1)_{12}$ model in this analysis must be written in terms of the regularly *and* seasonally differenced time series. Representing the Sutter County Workforce series by Y_t

$$Z_t = Y_t - Y_{t-1}$$

$$W_t = Z_t - Z_{t-12} = Y_t - Y_{t-1} - Y_{t-12} + Y_{t-13}$$

$$W_t = a_t - .60a_{t-1} - .68a_{t-12} + .408a_{t-13}$$

which describes the regularly and seasonally differenced series as the sum of a current shock (a_t), a portion of the preceding shock (a_{t-1}), a portion of the shock from the previous year (a_{t-12}), and a portion of the shock preceding that one (a_{t-13}). While this model may intimidate the reader at first, it is a surprisingly simple model which yet provides a surprisingly accurate picture of the time series process.

3.0 THE INTERVENTION COMPONENT, I_t

Having built a model of the time series process, the analyst may *use* that model to assess the impact of an exogenous intervention on the time series. Representing the $ARIMA(p,d,q)(P,D,Q)s$ model as N_t, the impact assessment model may be written as

$$Y_t = f(I_t) + N_t.$$

The "function of I_t," $f(I_t)$, is the intervention component of the model. Written in this form, the N_t component is the null case of the time series quasi-experiment. The Y_t time series is adequately explained as "noise" by the N_t component. If the intervention component increases the explanatory power of the model by a statistically significant quantity, the analyst may conclude that the exogenous intervention has had a statistically significant impact on the time series.

We use the term *impact assessment* to refer to the statistical analysis of a time series quasi-experiment. More generally, an impact assessment is "a test of the null hypothesis that a postulated event caused a change in a social process measured as a time series." Acknowledging the faults and limitations of this definition, we must immediately comment on its two key elements.

First, impact assessment is concerned with the effects of a "postulated event." An event for our purposes is a qualitative change in state or, in common terms, "something that happens." Events can be represented as binary variables which indicate the *absence* of the state prior to the event and the *presence* of the state during and (possibly) after the event. In the parlance of experimental psychology, for example, introduction of a treatment is the event associated with a change in state from "no treatment" to "treatment." In legal studies, enactment of a new law is the event associated with a change in state from "no regulation" to "regulation."

Qualitative changes in states (events) are often indistinguishable from quantitative changes in levels (processes). In studying national arms expenditures over time, for example, some social scientists prefer to think of "war" as an *event* which affects expenditures. Other social scientists prefer to think of "the propensity to war" as a continuous *process* which affects expenditures. Where the agent of change must be represented as a process (rather than as an event), multivariate ARIMA models are required (see McCleary and Hay, 1980: Chapter 5). We will cover only those situations here where the change agent is well represented by an event and, hence, those situations where a time series quasi-experiment is appropriate.

Because the change agent is an event, it is represented in the model as a "dummy" variable or step function such that

$$I_t = 0 \text{ prior to the event}$$
$$= 1 \text{ thereafter.}$$

The impact of this event, as represented by I_t, on the dependent variable, Y_t, will be determined by the particular "function of I_t" selected by the analyst. As we will soon demonstrate, a simple set of functions permits the analyst to model a wide variety of impacts.

A second element of the "impact assessment" definition is the a priori specification of the onset of an event. A null hypothesis that an event "caused" a change in some behavior can be tested only because the time of the event is known a priori. It would indeed be possible to search the length of a time series for statistically significantly changes but it would be logically impossible to then associate each change with the infinite number of events which might be the alleged causes. An impact analysis based on such a blind search might generously be called "exploratory analysis." Its results are quite uninterpretable. An impact assessment based on an event whose onset is specified a priori, in contrast, is a "confirmatory analysis." It is used only to test theoretically generated hypotheses according to a rigorous set of validity criteria.

Impact assessment (or the time series analysis of impacts) begins with an ARIMA model for the time series. Since this ARIMA model describes

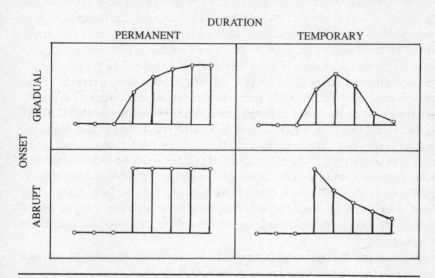

Figure 3a   Impact Patterns

the stochastic behavior of the time series process, we refer to it as the "noise component" of the impact assessment model. An "intervention component," $f(I_t)$, is then added to the model and, as we have noted, there are several distinct functions of I_t which correspond to several distinct *types* of impact.

In general, we have found it useful to think of an impact in terms of two characteristics: *onset* and *duration*. An impact on a social process may be either *abrupt* or *gradual* in onset and either *permanent* or *temporary* in duration. Figure 3a shows four patterns of impact which differ only in terms of onset and duration. Three of these four patterns are determined by simple intervention components. The fourth pattern— a *gradual, temporary* impact—cannot be modeled easily. This model would seem to be the least useful of the four, however. Ideally, the analyst will be able to select one of these impact patterns on the basis of theory, so the null hypothesis will center not only on the statistical significance of an impact but also on its form.

3.1 An Abrupt, Permanent Impact

The simplest possible intervention component is

$$f(I_t) = \omega I_t$$

where I_t is a step function and ω is a parameter to be estimated. The impact assessment model based on this intervention component is

$$Y_t = \omega I_t + N_t.$$

Now because this impact assessment model is linear in its components, the noise component may be subtracted from the time series.

$$y_t = Y_t - N_t$$
$$y_t = \omega I_t.$$

Working with the y_t series, we may observe the deterministic behavior of the intervention component without considering the stochastic behavior of the noise component.

Prior to the intervention, when $I_t = 0$, the level of the y_t series is zero.

$$y_t = \omega(0) = 0.$$

But postintervention, when $I_t = 1$, the level of the y_t series is

$$y_t = \omega(1) = \omega.$$

This simplest intervention component thus determines an *abrupt* and *permanent* shift in the level of a time series, something of the sort

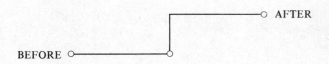

A few comments on the concept of "level" may be helpful here. An impact assessment model describes a change in level and/or (sometimes) trend for the generating process of the time series. Some writers use the term *equilbrium* rather than *level*, but whichever term is used, it is important to remember that a statistical (not a substantive) concept is implied.

For a stationary time series process, the parameter ω is an estimate of the difference between pre- and postintervention process levels. For a non-stationary series, an analogous interpretation is possible. An *abrupt, permanent* pattern of impact in a trending series may appear as

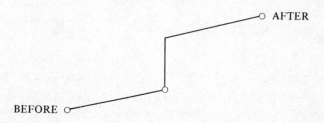

The interpretation of the ω parameter is more or less the same, then, whether the N_t component is a stationary $ARIMA(p,0,q)(P,0,Q)_s$ model or a nonstationary $ARIMA(p,d,q)(P,D,Q)_s$ model.

Using the simple intervention component, we will now demonstrate an impact assessment model-building strategy by analyzing the Directory Assistance time series which we introduced earlier (Figure 1a). In March 1974, the 147th month of this series, Cincinnati Bell initiated a $.20 charge for each call to Directory Assistance. Prior to this time, there was no charge for these calls. The impact of this event is visually striking. In the 147th month, the level of this time series drops abruptly and profoundly. When an impact is as large as the one in this example, the change in level complicates identification of the noise component. The change in level tends to overwhelm the ACF and PACF. To avoid biased estimates of the ACFs and PACFs, only the first 146 observations of the series will be used for identification. The ACFs and PACFs are shown in Figure 3.1a to 3.1d.

(1) *Identification.* The ACF and PACF estimated from the raw series (Figure 3.1a) indicate a nonstationary process; the series must be differenced. The ACF and PACF estimated from the regularly differenced series (Figure 3.1b) indicate that the series must be seasonally differenced as well. The ACF and PACF estimated from the regularly *and* seasonally differenced series (Figure 3.1c) suggest an $ARIMA(0,1,0)(0,1,1)_{12}$ model. For this model, the time series is differenced regularly

$$Z_t = Y_t - Y_{t-1}$$

and then seasonally

$$W_t = Z_t - Z_{t-1}$$

(or vice versa). The regularly *and* seasonally differenced series is then set equal to a 12th-order moving average.

$$W_t = \theta_0 + a_t - \theta_{12}a_{t-12}.$$

This is an interesting model and somewhat rare. The only autocorrelation is at seasonal lags of the series.

(2) *Estimation.* Parameter estimates for the N_t model are

$$\hat{\theta}_0 = -.70 \text{ with t statistic} = -1.51$$
$$\hat{\theta}_{12} = .85 \text{ with t statistic} = 15.30.$$

The estimate of θ_0 is not statistically significant, so it is dropped from the tentative model. The estimate of θ_{12} is statistically significant and lies within the bounds of invertibility.

(3) *Diagnosis.* The residual ACF and PACF (Figure 3.1d) indicate that the residuals of this model are not different than white noise. There is a significant spike at ACF(5) but nothing else; $Q = 12.52$ with 24 degrees of freedom is not statistically significant, so the tentative model is accepted.

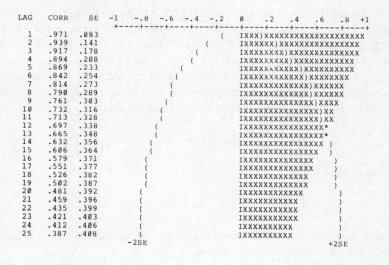

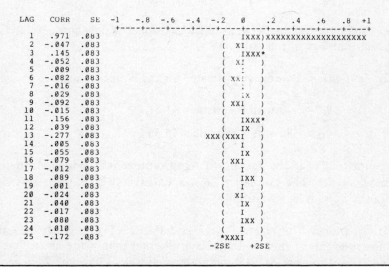

Figure 3.1a ACF and PACF for the Raw Directory Assistance Series

```
SERIES.. TEL146   (NOBS= 146)  DIRECTORY ASST - PRE INTERVENTION
DIFFERENCED  1 TIME(S) OF ORDER  1.
NO. OF VALID OBSERVATIONS  =   145.

AUTOCORRELATIONS OF LAGS 1 - 25.
Q( 25, 145) =  63.683     SIG =    .000


  LAG   CORR    SE   -1   -.8  -.6  -.4  -.2   0    .2   .4   .6   .8  +1
                     +----+----+----+----+----+----+----+----+----+----+
    1   .032   .083                         (   IX   )
    2  -.195   .083                        X(XXXI   )
    3   .053   .086                         (   IX   )
    4   .012   .086                         (   I    )
    5   .006   .086                         (   I    )
    6   .022   .086                         (   IX   )
    7  -.069   .087                         (  XXI   )
    8   .104   .087                         (   IXXX)
    9   .021   .088                         (   IX   )
   10  -.235   .088                       XX(XXXI   )
   11  -.017   .092                         (   I    )
   12   .360   .092                         (   IXXXX)XXXX
   13  -.014   .101                         (   I    )
   14  -.150   .101                        (XXXXI    )
   15   .026   .103                         (   IX   )
   16  -.045   .103                         (  XI    )
   17  -.058   .103                         (  XI    )
   18  -.010   .103                         (   I    )
   19  -.072   .103                         (  XXI   )
   20   .023   .104                         (   IX   )
   21   .045   .104                         (   IX   )
   22  -.239   .104                        X(XXXXI   )
   23  -.017   .107                         (   I    )
   24   .319   .107                         (   IXXXX)XXX
   25  -.002   .114                         (   I    )
                                          -2SE      +2SE


PARTIAL AUTOCORRELATIONS OF LAGS 1 - 25.


  LAG   CORR    SE   -1   -.8  -.6  -.4  -.2   0    .2   .4   .6   .8  +1
                     +----+----+----+----+----+----+----+----+----+----+
    1   .032   .083                         (   IX   )
    2  -.196   .083                        X(XXXI   )
    3   .070   .083                         (   IXX  )
    4  -.033   .083                         (  XI    )
    5   .033   .083                         (   IX   )
    6   .012   .083                         (   I    )
    7  -.065   .083                         (  XXI   )
    8   .123   .083                         (   IXXX)
    9  -.023   .083                         (  XI    )
   10  -.193   .083                        X(XXXI   )
   11  -.007   .083                         (   I    )
   12   .311   .083                         (   IXXX)XXXX
   13  -.038   .083                         (  XI    )
   14  -.069   .083                         (  XXI   )
   15   .020   .083                         (   I    )
   16  -.073   .083                         (  XXI   )
   17  -.089   .083                         (  XXI   )
   18  -.005   .083                         (   I    )
   19  -.033   .083                         (  XI    )
   20  -.082   .083                         (  XXI   )
   21   .026   .083                         (   IX   )
   22  -.116   .083                        (XXXI    )
   23   .003   .083                         (   I    )
   24   .179   .083                         (   IXXX*
   25   .016   .083                         (   I    )
                                          -2SE      +2SE
```

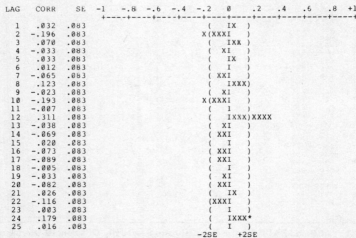

Figure 3.1b ACF and PACF for the Regularly Differenced Directory Assistance Series

```
SERIES.. TEL146   (NOBS= 146)  DIRECTORY ASST - PRE INTERVENTION
DIFFERENCED  1 TIME(S) OF ORDER  1.
DIFFERENCED  1 TIME(S) OF ORDER 12.
NO. OF VALID OBSERVATIONS  =   133.

AUTOCORRELATIONS OF LAGS 1 - 25.
Q( 25, 133) =  25.266      SIG =    .448


  LAG   CORR   SE  -1   -.8   -.6   -.4   -.2   0    .2   .4   .6   .8  +1
                     +----+----+----+----+----+----+----+----+----+----+
    1  -.036  .087                          (    XI   )
    2   .033  .087                          (    IX   )
    3   .083  .087                          (    IXX  )
    4   .009  .088                          (    I    )
    5   .087  .088                          (    IXX  )
    6   .073  .088                          (    IXX  )
    7   .021  .089                          (    IX   )
    8   .110  .089                          (    IXXX )
    9  -.034  .090                          (   XI    )
   10  -.023  .090                          (   XI    )
   11   .070  .090                          (    IXX  )
   12  -.294  .090                   XX (XXXXI       )
   13   .021  .097                          (    IX   )
   14  -.023  .097                          (   XI    )
   15  -.035  .097    -                     (   XI    )
   16  -.069  .097                          (  XXI    )
   17   .102  .098                          (    IXXX )
   18  -.121  .098                       ( XXXI       )
   19  -.061  .100                          (  XXI    )
   20  -.038  .100                          (   XI    )
   21   .116  .100                          (    IXXX )
   22  -.095  .101                          (  XXI    )
   23  -.038  .102                          (   XI    )
   24  -.015  .102                          (    I    )
   25   .032  .102                          (    IX   )
                                         -2SE      +2SE

PARTIAL AUTOCORRELATIONS OF LAGS 1 - 25.


  LAG   CORR   SE  -1   -.8   -.6   -.4   -.2   0    .2   .4   .6   .8  +1
                     +----+----+----+----+----+----+----+----+----+----+
    1  -.036  .087                          (   XI    )
    2   .031  .087                          (    IX   )
    3   .086  .087                          (    IXX  )
    4   .014  .087                          (    I    )
    5   .083  .087                          (    IXX  )
    6   .073  .087                          (    IXX  )
    7   .021  .087                          (    IX   )
    8   .096  .087                          (    IXX  )
    9  -.040  .087                          (   XI    )
   10  -.045  .087                          (   XI    )
   11   .042  .087                          (    IX   )
   12  -.305  .087                  XXXX (XXXI        )
   13  -.022  .087                          (   XI    )
   14  -.032  .087                          (   XI    )
   15   .004  .087                          (    I    )
   16  -.075  .087                          (  XXI    )
   17   .173  .087                          (    IXXX*
   18  -.069  .087                          (  XXI    )
   19  -.049  .087                          (   XI    )
   20   .025  .087                          (    IX   )
   21   .150  .087                          (    IXXX*
   22  -.133  .087                        (XXXI       )
   23   .002  .087                          (    I    )
   24  -.108  .087                        (XXXI       )
   25   .039  .087                          (    IX   )
                                         -2SE      +2SE
```

Figure 3.1c ACF and PACF for the Regularly and Seasonally Differenced Directory Assistance Series

```
SERIES.. RESIDUAL (NOBS= 133)  DIRECTORY ASST - PRE IMPACT RESIDUALS
NO. OF VALID OBSERVATIONS  =    133.

AUTOCORRELATIONS OF LAGS 1 - 25.
Q( 24, 133) =   12.522      SIG =      .973


   LAG   CORR    SE  -1   -.8  -.6  -.4  -.2   0    .2   .4   .6   .8  +1
                      +----+----+----+----+----+----+----+----+----+----+
    1   -.026   .087                          (   XI   )
    2    .009   .087                          (   I    )
    3    .089   .087                          (   IXX  )
    4   -.032   .087                          (   XI   )
    5    .165   .088                          (   IXXX*
    6    .029   .090                          (   IX   )
    7   -.041   .090                          (   XI   )
    8    .111   .090                          (  IXXX )
    9    .023   .091                          (   IX   )
   10   -.061   .091                          (  XXI   )
   11   -.033   .091                          (   XI   )
   12    .012   .092                          (   I    )
   13   -.051   .092                          (   XI   )
   14   -.001   .092                          (   I    )
   15   -.053   .092                          (   XI   )
   16   -.088   .092                          (  XXI   )
   17    .055   .093                          (   IX   )
   18   -.060   .093                          (   XI   )
   19   -.019   .093                          (   I    )
   20   -.014   .093                          (   I    )
   21    .087   .093                          (   IXX  )
   22   -.061   .094                          (  XXI   )
   23   -.064   .094                          (  XXI   )
   24   -.018   .094                          (   I    )
   25   -.029   .094                          (   XI   )
                                         -2SE       +2SE


PARTIAL AUTOCORRELATIONS OF LAGS 1 - 25.


   LAG   CORR    SE  -1   -.8  -.6  -.4  -.2   0    .2   .4   .6   .8  +1
                      +----+----+----+----+----+----+----+----+----+----+
    1   -.026   .087                          (   XI   )
    2    .008   .087                          (   I    )
    3    .089   .087                          (   IXX  )
    4   -.028   .087                          (   XI   )
    5    .164   .087                          (   IXXX*
    6    .029   .087                          (   IX   )
    7   -.037   .087                          (   XI   )
    8    .083   .087                          (  IXX )
    9    .033   .087                          (   IX   )
   10   -.083   .087                          (  XXI   )
   11   -.066   .087                          (  XXI   )
   12    .024   .087                          (   IX   )
   13   -.072   .087                          (  XXI   )
   14   -.018   .087                          (   I    )
   15   -.030   .087                          (   XI   )
   16   -.072   .087                          (  XXI   )
   17    .038   .087                          (   IX   )
   18   -.023   .087                          (   XI   )
   19    .009   .087                          (   I    )
   20   -.020   .087                          (   XI   )
   21    .139   .087                          (   IXXX)
   22   -.073   .087                          (  XXI   )
   23   -.062   .087                          (  XXI   )
   24   -.015   .087                          (   I    )
   25   -.023   .087                          (   XI   )
                                         -2SE       +2SE
```

Figure 3.1d   ACF for the Directory Assistance Model Residuals

As an aside, we note that another analyst might be concerned about the spike at ACF(5) which might indicate the need for a more elaborate model. Also, the estimated value of θ_0 is marginally significant and some other analyst might decide to keep that parameter in the model. The reader is invited to explore these possibilities.

(4) *Impact assessment.* The impact assessment model is tentatively set as

$$W_t = \omega I_{147} + a_t - \theta_{12} a_{t-12}$$

where

$$I_{147} = 0 \text{ for the first 146 observations}$$

$$= 1 \text{ for the 147th and subsequent observations.}$$

Parameter estimates for the tentative model are

$$\hat{\theta}_{12} = \quad .81 \text{ with t statistic} = \quad 11.21$$

$$\hat{\omega} = -39,931 \text{ with t statistic} = -17.41.$$

Both estimates are statistically significant and the estimate of θ_{12} lies within the bounds of invertibility.

Our interpretation of these findings is obvious. In the 147th month, the level of this series dropped by nearly 40,000 average daily calls to Directory Assistance.

The model-building strategy outlined in this example can be followed generally in all analyses. Each analysis will present a unique set of problems, however, which may require a slight adaptation of the strategy. In this case, for example, we had to use the preintervention segment for identification. We note finally that, in this example, a test of the null hypothesis was not at all in question. The impact was visually obvious. Impact assessment analysis nonetheless provided a precise estimate of the form and magnitude of the effect.

As an exercise, the reader should replicate this analysis. If the noise component of the impact assessment model is identified on the basis of the entire series (instead of on the basis of the preintervention series only), the analyst will arrive at a slightly different picture of the impact; and the model will be of a lower quality in all respects. The Directory Assistance time series is unusual in that the real impact is relatively great, thus accounting for a major portion of the series variance. In the other time series we will analyze here, the real impacts are considerably smaller and this will make our analysis simpler.

3.2 A Gradual, Permanent Impact

In our opinion, most social science impacts will be more gradual in onset than the Directory Assistant impact. A *gradual, permanent* impact can be modeled by adding a lagged value of the time series to the intervention component. Working in terms of the y_t series again, the intervention component is written as

$$y_t = \delta y_{t-1} + \omega I_t.$$

The δ parameter in this model *must* be a greater than zero but less than unity, that is

$$0 < \delta < +1.$$

These constraints on the δ parameter are called the "*bounds of system stability.*" If the δ parameter is not constrained to these bounds, the time series system is unstable. At a later point, we will demonstrate that system instability is analogous to process nonstationarity.

Prior to the intervention, when $I_t = 0$, the expected value of the y_t series in this model is zero:

$$y_t = \delta y_{t-1} + \omega(0) = 0.$$

But after the intervention, when $I_t = 1$, the level of the y_t time series is expected to be nonzero. Denoting the point of intervention as $t = i$,

$$y_{i-1} = \delta y_{i-2} + \omega(0) = 0$$
$$y_i = \delta y_{i-1} + \omega(1) = \omega.$$

In the next moment, the level of the y_t series changes again:

$$y_{i+1} = \delta y_i + \omega(1)$$
$$= \delta(\omega) + \omega = \delta\omega + \omega.$$

And the level of the y_t series continues to change with each passing moment:

$$y_{i+2} = \delta y_{i+1} + \omega(1)$$
$$= \delta(\delta\omega + \omega) + \omega(1) = \delta^2\omega + \delta\omega + \omega$$

$$y_{i+3} = \delta y_{i+2} + \omega(1)$$
$$= \delta(\delta^2\omega + \delta\omega + \omega) + \omega(1)$$
$$= \delta^3\omega + \delta^2\omega + \delta\omega + \omega$$

$$y_{i+n} = \delta y_{i+n-1} + \omega(1)$$
$$= \delta^n\omega + \delta^{n-1}\omega + \ldots + \delta^2\omega + \delta\omega + \omega.$$

The level of the y_t series increases (or decreases if the ω parameter is negative) with each passing moment. However, the increase from the nth to the $n+1^{st}$ moment is $\delta^n\omega$ which is a very small number, approximately zero. Thus, while the level of the y_t series continues to increase (or decrease if ω is negative) with each successive postintervention observation, successive increases (or decreases) become smaller and smaller. The impact on the y_t time series determined by this intervention component is thus of the sort

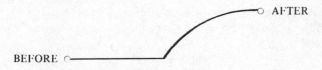

which is a *gradual* (but *permanent*) impact. Because the postintervention level of the y_t series continues to increase (although by smaller and smaller amounts), the asymptotic (or eventual) change in level is given by the infinite series

$$\text{asymptotic change in level} = \sum_{i=0}^{\infty} \delta^i\omega.$$

Because the δ parameter is smaller than unity, this infinite series converges and may be evaluated as

$$\text{asymptotic change in level} = \omega/(1 - \delta).$$

We will demonstrate shortly how this formula is interpreted. For the time being, however, it is more important to note that when δ is *not* a fraction (that is, when it does not satisfy the bounds of system stability), the formula is invalid.

While it is not immediately apparent, δ has a useful interpretation as a *rate* parameter. When δ is small, say $\delta = .1$, the asymptotic change in level is realized quite rapidly. When $\delta = 0$, of course, the change in level is instantaneous or *abrupt*. This follows from the fact that when $\delta = 0$, the intervention component reduces to

$$y_t = (0)y_{t-1} + \omega I_t = \omega I_t$$

which is the simple intervention component developed in Section 3.1. Finally, when δ is large, say $\delta = .9$, the asymptotic change in level is realized quite gradually.

Figure 3.2 shows the expected patterns of impact for several values of the δ parameter. A case of special interest is the case where $\delta = 1$. In this case, the postintervention series changes by a constant (ω) with each passing moment. An impact of this sort is interpreted as a postintervention *trend*; whereas prior to the intervention the y_t series was stationary, it is now nonstationary. Impacts of this sort would seem rare in the social sciences. The overwhelming majority of impacts should be well represented by the general intervention component where the value of δ is constrained to the interval

$$0 < \delta < 1$$

which are the bounds of system stability.

To demonstrate the use of this intervention component, we return to the Hyde Park purse snatchings time series. In the 41st period of this series, a community-whistle alert program was begun. This program would presumably have an impact on purse snatchings (a reduction, hopefully) but an abrupt impact would not be expected. Using the ARIMA (2,0,0) model identified previously, we estimate the parameters of the impact assessment model as

$$\hat{\phi}_1 = .242 \text{ with t statistic} = 2.03$$

$$\hat{\phi}_2 = .336 \text{ with t statistic} = 2.80$$

$$\hat{\delta} = .927 \text{ with t statistic} = 6.87$$

$$\hat{\omega} = -.781 \text{ with t statistic} = -.79.$$

Diagnostic checks applied to the residuals of this estimated model indicate that the residuals are white noise, so the model is accepted.

78

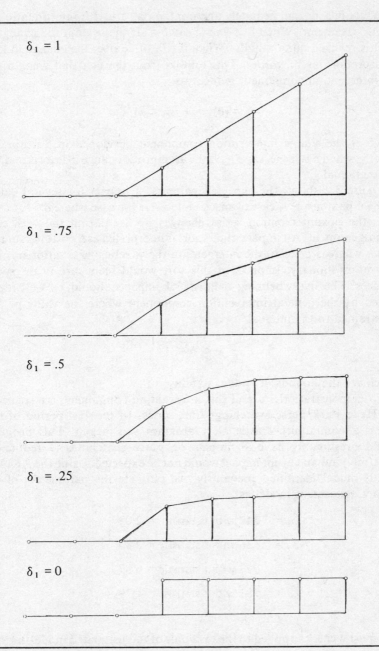

Figure 3.2   Gradual, Permanent Impact Patterns

Because the estimate of ω is not statistically significant, we will have to accept the null hypothesis: The community whistle-alert program had no impact on purse snatchings. For the time being, however, we will *interpret* these results without considering their statistical significance.

Working in terms of the y_t time series, the first postintervention observation is

$$y_{41} = .927y_{40} - .781(1) = -.781.$$

In other words, the level of the series *drops* by .781 purse snatchings in the first postintervention observation. In the second postintervention observation,

$$y_{42} = .927y_{41} - .781(1)$$
$$= .927(-.781) - .781 = -1.504.$$

And in successive postintervention observations,

$$y_{43} = .927y_{42} - .781(1)$$
$$= .927(-1.504) - .781 = -2.176$$
$$y_{44} = .927y_{43} - .781(1)$$
$$= .927(-2.176) - .781 = -2.798$$
$$y_{45} = .927y_4 - .781(1)$$
$$= .927(-2.798) - .781 = -3.375.$$

The level of the postintervention series continues to drop but by smaller and smaller amounts. In the nth postintervention observation,

$$y_{41+n} = .927y_{41+n-1} - .781(1)$$
$$= -.781[1 + .927 + (.927)^2 + \ldots + (.927)^{n-1}].$$

As n grows infinitely large, this level may be evaluated as

$$\text{asymptotic change} = -.781/(1 - .927) = -10.699.$$

The community whistle-alert program is thus expected to result in an eventual reduction of nearly 11 purse snatchings per reporting period. The change in level from period to period is quite small, however, so it will take a number of years for the program to achieve its full impact.

We note finally that this impact is not statistically different than zero. The interrupted time series quasi-experiment, however, like cross-sectional analyses, is sensitive to the amount of data used in the null hypothesis test. If a few dozen more postintervention observations were available here, it is quite possible that the estimated impact would be statistically significant.

3.3 An Abrupt, Temporary Impact

An abrupt, temporary pattern of impact is determined by representing the event with a *pulse* function (rather than a step function). The pulse function, P_t, is defined as

$P_t = 0$ prior to the intervention

$= 1$ at the moment of intervention

$= 0$ thereafter.

When the event is represented by a step function, the change in state is explicitly permanent. When the event is represented by a pulse function, however, the change in state is explicitly temporary; it endures for only one moment.

Working in terms of the y_t time series, an intervention component for an abrupt, temporary impact model is

$$y_t = \delta y_{t-1} + \omega P_t.$$

Prior to intervention, when $P_t = 0$, the level of the y_t series is expected to be zero. But at the moment of intervention, $t = i$ and $P_i = 1$,

$$y_i = \delta y_{i-1} + \omega P_i$$
$$= \delta(0) + \omega(1) = \omega.$$

In the next postintervention moment, $P_{i+1} = 0$, so

$$y_{i+1} = \delta y_i + \omega P_{i+1}$$
$$= \delta(\omega) + \omega(0) = \delta\omega.$$

And in the next postintervention moment

$$y_{i+2} = \delta y_{i+1} + \omega P_{i+2}$$
$$= \delta(\delta\omega) + \omega(0) = \delta^2\omega.$$

A progression begins to emerge. In the nth postintervention moment,

$$y_{i+n} = \delta y_{i+n-1} + \omega P_{i+n}$$
$$= \delta(\delta^{n-1}\omega) + \omega(0) = \delta^{n}\omega.$$

Because the δ parameter is constrained to the bounds of system stability, the term $\delta^{n}\omega$ will be quite small, approximately zero. The intervention component thus describes a spike, beginning at the moment of intervention, and decaying across the postintervention segment. This impact is of the sort

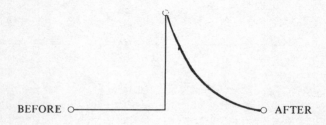

There are a number of temporary social phenomena which are expected to have impacts of this sort.

Figure 3.3 shows the expected patterns of impact for several values of this *rate* parameter. When δ is small, say $\delta = .1$, the postintervention series level decays rapidly back to its preintervention level. When δ is large, say $\delta = .9$, the spike decays slowly. Finally, when $\delta = 1$, the spike does not decay but remains constant throughout the postintervention period. We will make use of this property at a later point.

To demonstrate how this intervention component is used, we return to the Sutter County Workforce time series (Figure 1b). In January 1955, the 121st observation of this series, a flood forced the evacuation of Sutter County. Friesema et al. (1979) used an abrupt, temporary model of impact to assess the economic recovery of Sutter County from the flood. Like the pulse function, a natural disaster is abrupt in onset and short in duration. Even though a natural disaster is short-lived, however, its impact remains for some time afterward. One advantage to using an abrupt, temporary model in this context is that the δ parameter can be interpreted as the *rate* of recovery during the disaster aftermath.

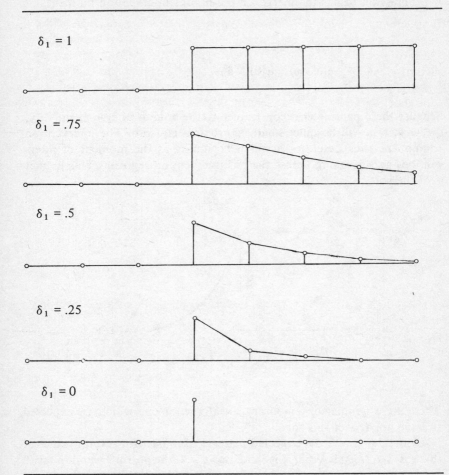

$\delta_1 = 1$

$\delta_1 = .75$

$\delta_1 = .5$

$\delta_1 = .25$

$\delta_1 = 0$

Figure 3.3   Abrupt, Temporary Impact Patterns

Using the ARIMA$(0,1,1)(0,1,1)_{12}$ model identified previously, parameter estimates for the impact assessment model are

$$\hat{\theta}_1 = \qquad .60 \text{ with t statistic} = 11.38$$

$$\hat{\theta}_{12} = \qquad .68 \text{ with t statistic} = 13.33$$

$$\hat{\delta} = \qquad .84 \text{ with t statistic} = \quad 2.64$$

$$\hat{\omega} = -267.44 \text{ with t statistic} = -1.36.$$

All parameter estimates except the estimate of ω are statistically significant and otherwise acceptable. A diagnostic check of the residuals indicates that they are not different than white noise, so the model is accepted.

According to Friesema et al., the economy of Sutter County is largely agricultural and, as the flood struck in December after the end of the normal growing season, there was little disruption to the local economy. By the start of the next growing season, there was little unrepaired damage to farmlands. Using the estimated values of δ and ω, a "best estimate" of the flood's impact on the workforce time series is

January 1956:   displacement $= (.84)^0(-276.44) = -276.44$

February 1956:   displacement $= (.84)^1(-276.44) = -232.21$

March 1956:   displacement $= (.84)^2(-276.44) = -195.06$

April 1956:   displacement $= (.84)^3(-276.44) = -163.85$

December 1956:   displacement $= (.84)^{11}(-276.44) = -40.61$

and so forth. A year after the flood, the workforce time series had returned (more or less) to its preflood level.

These displacement figures are given in worker-months, the metric of the workforce time series. To estimate the total number of worker-months lost due to the flood, the infinite series

$$\sum_{i=0}^{\infty} (.84)^i(-276.44)$$

can be evaluated with the formula

total displacement $= -276.44/(1 - .84) = -1727.75$ worker-months.

This total is interpreted as the sum of all worker-months lost in the flood's aftermath. Geometrically, this number is the area under the decaying spike. As there are approximately 36,000 worker-months in an average year of this time series, the impact of the flood on the Sutter County Workforce time series is substantively trivial.

3.4 Testing Rival Hypotheses

In preceding sections, we developed three intervention components, each associated with a distinct pattern of impact. These include an abrupt, permanent pattern of impact associated with the component

$$f(I_t) = \omega I_t;$$

a gradual, permanent pattern of impact associated with the component

$$f(I_t) = \delta Y_{t-1} + \omega I_t;$$

and an abrupt, temporary pattern of impact associated with the component

$$f(I_t) = \delta Y_{t-1} + \omega P_t.$$

In an ideal situation, the analyst will work from a body of theory which points to one of these three patterns of impact and, thus, to one of the three intervention components. Where theory is lacking, however, logical relationships between the three intervention components permits the analyst to test rival impact hypotheses.

To illustrate these relationships, first consider the behavior of the abrupt, temporary intervention component at the bounds of system stability. Referring to Figure 3.3, it is clear that recovery is instantaneous whenever $\delta = 0$. When $\delta = 1$, however, there is no recovery at all. In fact, while we will not do so here, it can be demonstrated that, when $\delta = 1$, the abrupt, temporary intervention component and the abrupt, permanent intervention component are identical. Similarly, referring to Figure 3.2, it is clear that, when $\delta = 0$, the gradual, permanent intervention component and the abrupt, permanent intervention component are identical.

These relationships suggest a rather simple method for checking the appropriateness of an intervention component. First, if the analyst has no a priori notions about the expected pattern of impact, the analysis can start with the abrupt, temporary intervention component. If the estimated value of δ is "too large," near unity, a temporary impact is ruled out. Next, the analyst hypothesizes a gradual, permanent impact. If the estimated value of δ is "too small," not significantly different than zero, a gradual impact is ruled out. The only pattern of impact remaining is an abrupt, permanent pattern.

To illustrate this procedure, we return to the Directory Assistance time series. Eyeballing the plotted series (Figure 1a), there is no doubt that the impact is abrupt and permanent. But suppose now that the appropriate intervention component is unknown. The "blind" analysis begins with the abrupt, temporary component. Estimates of the impact parameters are

$$\hat{\delta} = .99295 \text{ with t statistic} = 70.64$$

$$\hat{\omega} = -38,034 \text{ with t statistic} = -13.47.$$

The estimate of δ is clearly "too large" to support the hypothesis of a temporary impact. A 95% confidence interval about this estimate lies well beyond the bounds of system stability.

As a second step in the blind analysis, a gradual, permanent component is incorporated into the model. Estimates of the impact parameters are

$$\hat{\delta} = -.0396 \text{ with t statistic} = -.56$$

$$\hat{\omega} = 37,900 \text{ with t statistic} = -13.38.$$

This estimate of δ is clearly too small to support the hypothesis of a gradual impact. Because two of the three intervention components (and hence, two of the three impact patterns) have been ruled out, only the abrupt, permanent pattern of impact remains a plausible hypothesis.

4.0 CONCLUSION

Box-Tiao models for the time series quasi-experiment begin with a noise component, an ARIMA model for the time series. The procedures by which the ARIMA model is built have been outlined as a flow-chart in Figure 2.7a. Within reason, this model-building strategy can be followed mechanically to arrive at an ARIMA model that is statistically adequate (its residuals are white noise) and parsimonious (it has the fewest parameters and the greatest number of degrees of freedom among all statistically adequate models). To be sure, there are a number of alternative model-building strategies that could be followed. These alternative strategies will not generally lead to a model that is both statistically adequate and parsimonious, however.

Having built a satisfactory noise component for the time series, the analyst next selects an appropriate intervention component which is coupled additively to the noise component. This full impact assessment model may be written as

$$Y_t = f(I_t) + N_t.$$

We have described three simple intervention components, each associated with a distinct pattern of impact. Ideally, the analyst will have an a priori notion of the expected impact; it may be abrupt or gradual in onset, for example, and permanent or temporary in duration. There are a number of advantages to using these three intervention components. They are parsimonious (containing no more than two parameters), they have been widely used and thus tested in practice, and they seem to describe a wide variety of empirical social impact phenomena. An added advantage is that the three models are related logically and thus give a basis for testing rival impact hypotheses.

Once a satisfactory impact assessment model has been built (its parameters estimated, that is, and its residuals diagnosed), the analyst must *interpret* the results. In much of the quasi-experimental literature, interpretation consists only of testing a null hypothesis: Did the intervention have a statistically significant impact on a time series? In many cases, however, an adequate interpretation of the analysis will require some statement as to the *form* of the impact. Was it abrupt or gradual, permanent or temporary? If gradual in onset, how gradual? All of these questions can be answered by interpreting the model parameter estimates.

The general model-building strategy will require some minor modification in rare cases. In the Directory Assistance time series, for example, the impact was so large that ACFs and PACFs had to be estimated from the preintervention series only. ACFs and PACFs estimated from the entire series would be overwhelmed and distorted by the real impact in the series. The Hyde Park purse snatching series and the Sutter County Workforce series, on the other hand, had relatively minor impacts, so the noise component could be identified from ACFs and PACFs estimated over the entire series. In our opinion, most social impacts will be of this magnitude and, hence, will present few practical problems in identification. The analyst nevertheless must exercise common sense on this point.

Our presentation of time series analysis in this essay has assumed that the reader will practice these methods and, indeed, this is the only way to fully learn time series analysis. In the past, time series methods have not been widely used by social scientists largely because the required software has not been accessible. This is no longer the case. Nearly all academic computing centers now maintain a number of Box-Tiao and/or Box-Jenkins software packages. As of the spring of 1980, all of the major statistical analysis systems (BMDP, MINITAB, SAS, and SPSS) include ARIMA time series analysis programs. We assume that all academic computing centers will have at least one of these four statistical analysis systems; most will have more than one; and many academic computing centers will have all four.

In addition to these comprehensive systems, there are two stand-alone packages which are widely available at university computing centers. PACK (Pack, 1977) is a general Box-Jenkins program. We have found this program to be extremely flexible and economical. Its major disadvantage is that it assumes a high level of sophistication; it is not well-suited to classroom use. It is an excellent program for anyone planning a major time series research project, however. The other widely available stand-alone package is TMS (Bower et al., 1974). This program is now generally considered to be obsolete and cannot be recommended either for classroom use or for research. It can accommodate only nonseasonal ARIMA models and a narrow set of intervention components. Furthermore, TMS has an inefficient estimation algorithm which makes its use prohibitively expensive.

For classroom use, the BMDP system is recommended. The BMDP ARIMA time series program (BMDP2T) shares file structure and syntax with other BMDP programs, so most students will have little difficulty using this program. In addition, BMDP2T can be run interactively. MINITAB, SAS, and SPSS time series programs (*at this time:* spring of 1980) are not as well-developed as the BMDP program. Development in this area proceeds rapidly, however, so it is likely that these other systems will be greatly improved within the near future. In Appendix A, we list the addresses of major time series software distributors. The reader is urged to contact these distributors for information on current offerings.

APPENDIX A

ARIMA Time Series Software Distributors

Program	Distributor
BMDP2T	Health Science Computing Facility Department of Biomathematics University of California Los Angeles, CA 90024
IMSL	International Mathematical and Statistical Libraries, Inc. 7500 Bellaire Boulevard Houston, TX 77036
MINITAB	Professor Thomas A. Ryan Statistics Department 215 Pond Laboratory The Pennsylvania State University University Park, PA 16802
PACK	Automatic Forecasting Systems P.O. Box 563 Hatboro, PA 19040
SAS	SAS Institute, Inc. P.O. Box 10066 Raleigh, NC 27605
SPSS	SPSS, Inc. Suite 3300 444 North Michigan Avenue Chicago, IL 60611

APPENDIX B

Average Daily Calls to Directory Assistance, Cincinnati, OH; 180 monthly observations, January 1962–December 1976; source: Dr. A.J. McSweeny, Department of Psychology, University of West Virginia; see McSweeney (1978).

350	339	351	364	369	331	331	340	346	341	357	398
381	367	383	375	353	361	375	371	373	366	382	429
406	403	429	425	427	409	402	409	419	404	429	463
428	449	444	467	474	463	432	453	462	456	474	514
489	475	492	525	527	533	527	522	526	513	564	599
572	587	599	601	611	620	579	582	592	581	630	663
638	631	645	682	601	595	521	521	516	496	538	575
537	534	542	538	547	540	526	548	555	545	594	643
625	616	640	625	637	634	621	641	654	649	662	699
672	704	700	711	715	718	652	664	695	704	733	772
716	712	732	755	761	748	748	750	744	731	782	810
777	816	840	868	872	811	810	762	634	626	649	697
657	549	162	177	175	162	161	165	170	172	178	186
178	178	189	205	202	185	193	200	196	204	206	227
225	217	219	236	253	213	205	210	216	218	235	241

APPENDIX C

Sutter County Workforce; 252 monthly observations, January 1946–December 1966; source: Friesema et al. (1979).

890	992	979	959	1110	1546	1539	3401	2092	1436	1301	1287
1488	1517	1707	1729	1788	2008	2203	3713	2946	2082	2033	1937
1711	1775	1902	1846	2083	2262	2193	3792	2343	2313	2179	1975
1880	1930	2060	1843	2052	2039	2351	3394	3581	2489	2468	2134
1903	1719	1617	1818	2067	2457	2600	3530	2693	2448	2250	1972
1682	1730	1814	1900	2051	2290	2599	3428	2262	2242	2103	1825
1670	1681	1713	1954	1976	2272	2612	3590	2496	2441	2340	2090
1812	1788	1837	1993	2021	2199	2622	3787	2914	2487	2314	2139
2124	2214	2234	2279	2423	2290	2903	4485	3085	2852	2629	2435
2227	1944	2125	2260	2299	2323	2659	3761	2779	2761	2446	2278
1879	1881	2165	2199	2308	2529	2573	3946	3200	2574	2422	2446
2828	2879	2800	2835	2585	2787	3334	4746	3613	3463	3274	2801
2488	2386	2428	2678	2744	2772	3520	3833	3377	3013	2871	2592
2375	2304	2464	2557	2739	2714	3102	3961	3772	3245	3104	2869
2513	2385	2756	2927	2940	3180	3791	4093	4309	3532	3408	2839
2792	2798	3007	3086	3201	3428	3754	4917	3760	3609	3471	3347
3333	3456	3569	3900	3909	4098	4826	5770	5108	4360	4100	3562
3284	3278	3424	3843	3614	3536	4505	5456	4881	4041	3724	3525
3437	3324	3977	4025	4016	4031	4489	5563	5709	4620	4160	4012
3987	4155	4054	4485	4558	4462	4594	6481	6345	5142	4824	4573
4158	4140	4251	4734	4858	4798	5080	6905	5504	5457	5198	4890

APPENDIX D

Closing Price of IBM Common Stock, "Series B"; 369 daily observations, May 17, 1961–November 2, 1962; source: Box and Jenkins (1976).

460	457	452	459	462	459	463	479	493	490
492	498	499	497	496	490	489	478	487	491
487	482	479	478	479	477	479	475	479	476
476	478	479	477	476	475	475	473	474	474
474	465	466	467	471	471	467	473	481	488
490	489	489	485	491	492	494	499	498	500
497	494	495	500	504	513	511	514	510	509
515	519	523	519	523	531	547	551	547	541
545	549	545	549	547	543	540	539	532	517
527	540	542	538	541	541	547	553	559	557
557	560	571	571	569	575	580	584	585	590
599	603	599	596	585	587	585	581	583	592
592	596	596	595	598	598	595	595	592	588
582	576	578	589	585	580	579	584	581	581
577	577	578	580	586	583	581	576	571	575
575	573	577	582	584	579	572	577	571	560
549	556	557	563	564	567	561	559	553	553
553	547	550	544	541	532	525	542	555	558
551	551	552	553	557	557	548	547	545	545
539	539	535	537	535	536	537	543	548	546
547	548	549	553	553	552	551	550	553	554
551	551	545	547	547	537	539	538	533	525
513	510	521	521	521	523	516	511	518	517
520	519	519	519	518	513	499	485	454	462
473	482	486	475	459	451	453	446	455	452
457	449	450	435	415	398	399	361	383	393

APPENDIX E

Hyde Park Purse Snatchings; 71 28-day periods, January 1969–September 1973; source: Reed (1978).

10	15	10	10	12	10	7	17	10	14	8	17
14	18	3	9	11	10	6	12	14	10	25	29
33	33	12	19	16	19	19	12	34	15	36	29
26	21	17	19	13	20	24	12	6	14	6	12
9	11	17	12	8	14	14	12	5	8	10	3
16	8	8	7	12	6	10	8	10	5	7	

NOTES

1. In what follows, we will assume that the Y_t process has a zero mean. This is not an overly restrictive assumption, for if the Y_t process has a nonzero mean, we can work with the deviate time series, $Y_t - \theta_0$, where θ_0 is the nonzero mean of Y_t.

2. For those interested in somewhat more detail:

$$\text{covariance}(Y_t Y_{t+1}) = E[(a_t - \theta_1 a_{t-1})(a_{t+1} - \theta_1 a_t)]$$
$$= E(a_t a_{t+1} - \theta_1 a_t^2 - \theta_1 a_{t-1} a_{t+1} + \theta_1^2 a_{t-1} a_t)$$

where E is the expectation operator, meaning "the expected value of." Now by definition,

$$E(a_t) = \text{mean}(a_t) = 0$$
$$E(a_t^2) = \text{variance}(a_t) = \sigma^2$$
$$E(a_t a_{t+k}) = \text{covariance}(a_t a_{t+k}) = 0$$

so

$$\text{covariance}(Y_t Y_{t+1}) = E a_t a_{t+1} - \theta_1 E a_t^2 - \theta_1 E a_{t-1} a_{t+1} + \theta_1^2 E a_{t-1} a_t$$
$$= 0 - \theta_1 \sigma^2 - 0 + 0 = -\theta_1 \sigma^2.$$

McCleary and Hay (1980: Section 2.8) develop these expected ACFs in more detail.

3. In more detail:

$$\text{variance}(Y_t) = E[(a_t - \theta_1 a_{t-1})^2]$$
$$= E(a_t^2 - 2\theta_1 a_t a_{t-1} + \theta_1^2 a_{t-1}^2)$$
$$= E a_t^2 - 2\theta_1 E a_t a_{t-1} + \theta_1^2 E a_{t-1}^2$$
$$= \sigma^2(1 + \theta_1^2).$$

91

4. In more detail:

$$\text{covariance}(Y_t Y_{t+2}) = E[(a_t - \theta_1 a_{t-1})(a_{t+2} - \theta_1 a_{t+1})]$$

$$= E(a_t a_{t+2} - \theta_1 a_t a_{t+1} - \theta_1 a_{t-1} a_{t+2} + \theta_1^2 a_{t-1} a_{t+1})$$

$$= E a_t a_{t+2} - \theta_1 E a_t a_{t+1} - \theta_1 E a_{t-1} a_{t+2} + \theta_1^2 E a_{t-1} a_{t+1}$$

$$= 0 - 0 - 0 + 0 = 0.$$

5. Although nothing new is involved here, the derivation requires tedious arithmetic. The interested (or skeptical) reader may demonstrate it as an exercise.

6. In more detail:

$$\text{covariance}(Y_t Y_{t+1}) = E[Y_t(\phi_1 Y_t + a_{t+1})]$$

$$= E(\phi_1 Y_t^2 + Y_t a_{t+1})$$

$$= \phi_1 E Y_t^2 + E Y_t a_{t+1}$$

$$= \phi_1 \text{ variance}(Y_t) + 0.$$

7. In more detail:

$$\text{covariance}(Y_t Y_{t+2}) = E[(Y_t(\phi_1 Y_{t+1} + a_{t+2})]$$

$$= E\{Y_t[\phi_1(\phi_1 Y_t + a_{t+1}) + a_{t+2}]\}$$

$$= \phi_1^2 E Y_t^2 + \phi_1 E Y_t a_{t+1} + E Y_t a_{t+2}$$

$$= \phi_1^2 \text{ variance}(Y_t).$$

8. The PACF is estimated from the Yule-Walker equations. See Box and Jenkins (1976: 82-84) for a description of the actual estimation procedure. Standard errors for the PACF(k) are given by $\text{SE}[\text{PACF}(k)] = N^{-\frac{1}{2}}$ for an N-observation time series.

9. An ARIMA(p,0,0) process can be written as

$$Y_t = \phi_1 Y_{t-1} + \ldots + \phi_p Y_{t-p} + a_t.$$

Multiplying this expression by Y_{t-k} gives

$$Y_t Y_{t-k} = \phi_1 Y_{t-1} Y_{t-k} + \phi_p Y_{t-p} Y_{t-k} + a_t Y_{t-k}.$$

Taking the expected value of this expression and dividing by variance (Y_t)

$$\text{ACF}(k) = \phi_1 \text{ACF}(k-1) + \ldots + \phi_p \text{ACF}(k-p).$$

This relationship may be used to derive the expected ACFs for higher order autoregressive processes. To use this relationship, note that $\text{ACF}(0) = 1$ and $\text{ACF}(-k) = \text{ACF}(k)$.

10. This infinite series can be derived by substitution. Write out two observations of the ARIMA$(1,0,1)$ process as

$$Y_t = \phi_1 Y_{t-1} + a_t - \theta_1 a_{t-1}$$
$$Y_{t-1} = \phi_1 Y_{t-2} + a_{t-1} - \theta_1 a_{t-2}.$$

Then by substitution,

$$Y_t = \phi_1(\phi_1 Y_{t-2} + a_{t-1} - \theta_1 a_{t-2}) + a_t - \theta_1 a_{t-1}$$
$$= \phi_1^2 Y_{t-2} + a_t + (\phi_1 - \theta_1)a_{t-1} - \phi_1 \theta_1 a_{t-2}.$$

Substituting for Y_{t-2},

$$Y_t = \phi_1^2(\phi_1 Y_{t-3} + a_{t-2} - \theta_1 a_{t-3}) + a_t + (\phi_1 - \theta_1)a_{t-1} - \phi_1 \theta_1 a_{t-2}$$
$$= \phi_1^3 Y_{t-3} + a_t + (\phi_1 - \theta_1)a_{t-1} + \phi_1(\phi_1 - \theta_1)a_{t-2} - \phi_1^2 \theta_1 a_{t-3}.$$

Continuing this substitution indefinitely leads to the infinite series as given.

REFERENCES

AARONSON, D., C. T. DIENES, and M. C. MUSHENO (1978) "Changing the public drunkenness laws: The impact of decriminalization." Law and Society Review 12: 405-436.

BOWER, C. P., W. L. PADIA, and G. V GLASS (1974) TMS: Two FORTRAN IV Programs for Analysis of Time Series Experiments. Boulder: University of Colorado, Laboratory of Educational Research.

BOX, G.E.P. and G. M. JENKINS (1976) Time Series Analysis: Forecasting and Control. San Francisco: Holden-Day.

BOX, G.E.P. and G. C. TIAO (1975) "Intervention analysis with applications to economic and environmental problems." Journal of the American Statistical Association 70: 70-92.

——— (1965) "A change in level of a nonstationary time series." Biometrika 52: 181-192.

CAMPBELL, D. T. (1963) "From description to experimentation: Interpreting trends as quasi-experiments." In C. W. Harris (ed.), Problems of Measuring Change. Madison: University of Wisconsin Press.

——— and H. L. ROSS (1968) "The Connecticut crackdown on speeding: Time series data in quasi-experimental analysis." Law and Society Review 3: 33-53.

CAMBELL, J. T. and J. C. STANLEY (1966) Experimental and Quasi-Experimental Designs for Research. Skokie, IL: Rand McNally.

CAPORASO, J. A. and A. L. PELOWSKI (1971) "Economic and political integration in Europe: A time series quasi-experimental analysis." American Political Science Review 65: 418-433.

DEUTSCH, S. J. and F. B. ALT (1977) "The effect of Massachusetts' gun control law on gun-related crimes in the city of Boston." Evaluation Quarterly 1: 543-568.

FRIESEMA, H. P., J. CAPORASO, G. GOLDSTEIN, and R. McCLEARY (1979) Aftermath: Communities After Natural Disaster. Beverly Hills, CA: Sage.

GLASS, G. V (1968) "Analysis of data on the Connecticut speeding crackdown as a time series quasi-experiment." Law and Society Review 3: 55-76.

——— V. L. WILLSON, and J. M. GOTTMAN (1975) Design and Analysis of Time Series Experiments. Boulder: Colorado Associated Universities Press.

GOTTMAN, J. M. and R. M. McFALL (1972) "Self-monitoring effects in a program for potential high school dropouts: A time series analysis." Journal of Consulting and Clinical Psychology 39: 273-281.

HALL, R. V., R. FOX, D. WILLARD, L. GOLDSMITH, M. EMERSON, M. OWEN, F. DAVIS, and E. PORCIA (1971) "The teacher as observer and experimenter in the modification of disputing and talking-out behaviors." Journal of Applied Behavior Analysis 4: 141-149.

HAY, R. A., Jr. (1979) Interactive Analysis of Interrupted Time Series Models Using SCRUNCH. Evanston, IL: Northwestern University, Department of Sociology and Vogelback Computing Center.

———— and R. McCLEARY (1979) "Box-Tiao time series models for impact assessment: A comment on the recent work of Deutsch and Alt." Evaluation Quarterly 3: 277-314.

HIBBS, D. A., Jr. (1974) "Problems of statistical estimation and causal inference in time series regression models. In H. L. Costner (ed.), Sociological Methodology 1973-74. San Francisco: Jossey-Bass.

LEWIS-BECK, M. S. (1979) "Some economic effects of revolution: Models, measurement, and the Cuban evidence." American Journal of Sociology 84: 1127-1149.

McCLEARY, R. and R. A. HAY, Jr. with E. E. MEIDINGER and D. McDOWALL (1980) Applied Time Series Analysis for the Social Sciences. Beverly Hills, CA: Sage.

McCLEARY, R. and M. C. MUSHENO (1980) "Floor effects in the time series quasi-experiment." Political Methodology 7: 3.

McSWEENY, A. J. (1978) "The effects of response cost on the behavior of a million persons: Charging for directory assistance in Cincinnati." Journal of Applied Behavioral Analysis 11: 47-51.

OSTROM, C. W., Jr. (1978) Time Series Analysis: Regression Techniques. Sage University Papers Series on Quantitative Applications in the Social Sciences, 07-009. Beverly Hills, CA: Sage.

PACK, D. J. (1977) A Computer Program for the Analysis of Time Series Models Using the Box-Jenkins Philosophy. Columbus: Ohio State University, Data Center.

REED, D. (1978) Whistlestop: A Community Alternative for Crime Prevention. Ph.D. dissertation, Evanston, IL: Department of Sociology, Northwestern University.

ROSS, H. L., D. T. CAMPBELL, and G. V GLASS (1970) "Determining the effects of a legal reform: The British "breathalyzer" crackdown of 1967." American Behavioral Scientist 13: 493-509.

SMOKER, P. (1969) "A time series analysis of Sino-Indian relations." Journal of Conflict Resolution 13: 105-113.

TYLER, V. D. and G. D. BROWN (1968) "Token reinforcement of academic performance with institutionalized delinquent boys." Journal of Educational Psychology 59: 164-168.

ZIMRING, F. E. (1975) "Firearms and federal law: The gun control act of 1968." Journal of Legal Studies 4: 133-198.

DAVID McDOWALL is Postdoctoral Fellow at the Center for Research on Social Organization, University of Michigan. His Ph.D. is in sociology from Northwestern University. His research interests and publications are in the areas of quantitative methodology and criminology.

RICHARD McCLEARY is Associate Professor of Criminal Justice at Arizona State University. His Ph.D. is in sociology from Northwestern University. He has written several books and articles on applied time series analysis.

ERROL E. MEIDINGER is Senior Fellow at the Natural Resources Law Center of Lewis and Clark University. His research interests and publications are in the social impacts of economic decisions, particularly those which allocate natural resources among alternative uses.

RICHARD A. HAY, Jr., is on the staff of Vogelback Computing Center and is a Ph.D. candidate in sociology at Northwestern University. His research interests are in applied quantitative methodology and the political economy of socioeconomic development. He recently edited (with Janet Abu-Lughod) a volume of readings entitled Third World Urbanization *(Methuen).*